Design: David Houghton

Printed by: MPG Books, Bodmin

Published by: Sanctuary Publishing Limited, Sanctuary House, 45-53 Sinclair Road, London
W14 0NS, United Kingdom. Web site: www.sanctuarypublishing.com

Copyright: Paul White, 1999
Sound On Sound web site: www.sospubs.co.uk

ISBN: 1-86074-262-9

basic MIDI

PAUL WHITE

Also by Paul White from Sanctuary Publishing

Creative Recording I – Effects & Processors
Creative Recording II – Microphones, Acoustics,
    Soundproofing & Monitoring
Home Recording Made Easy
MIDI For The Technophobe
Live Sound For The Performing Musician
Recording & Production Techniques
Music Technology – A Survivor's Guide

Also in this series

basic DIGITAL RECORDING
basic EFFECTS AND PROCESSORS
basic HOME STUDIO DESIGN
basic LIVE SOUND
basic MASTERING
basic MICROPHONES
basic MULTITRACKING
basic MIXERS
basic MIXING TECHNIQUES

contents

chapter 1

....

chapter 2

chapter 3

chapter 4

chapter 5

....

MIDI SYNCHRONISATION   117

chapter 6

METHODS OF SYNTHESIS   **135**

chapter 7

introduction

MIDI has had a greater effect on the way we create and record music than almost any other development since the introduction of the tape recorder. The affordability of MIDI equipment means that a vast number of musicians are now able to create and record their own music without needing to use traditional recording studios, though understanding what MIDI is capable of and how to use it is something that scares off a lot of potential users.

My first experiences with MIDI were far from comfortable, and the main problem seemed to be the books that purported to explain the subject! They'd invariably dive in with explanations of bits, bytes, data structure and so on, when all I wanted to know was how to use MIDI.

After buying my first MIDI system and playing about with it for a few days, I was surprised at how straightforward and logical everything was – but I was even more surprised by the fact that I hadn't needed to know more than a tiny fraction of what the current books on MIDI implied that I needed to know. The purpose of this book, therefore, is to explore the applications of MIDI in as straightforward and practical a manner as possible by using analogies with familiar everyday processes. In this way you'll have a working knowledge of what goes on in a MIDI system, you'll know what you can expect to achieve and you'll also know how to go about achieving it, all in a very short space of time. After that, you can learn the more complex stuff at your leisure – if you ever feel the need to!

chapter 1

introducing MIDI

Most musicians have heard of MIDI ('it's something to do with computers and synthesisers isn't it?') but what exactly is it? What can it do for your music? And what equipment do you need to get started? While it's very tempting to jump straight in and start talking about MIDI synthesisers, soundcards, keyboards and interfaces, it's important to first create an overview of MIDI and find out what it is all about. To do that we have to wind the clock back to the early Eighties, when the major manufacturers of synthesisers got together and agreed on a standard system by which their different models of electronic instruments could be connected together as part of the same system. They called this the Musical Instrument Digital Interface, or MIDI for short.

Rather than overwhelming you with an avalanche of information and then making you dig your way out, I'm going to try to explain the general concept of MIDI in terms with which you are already familiar, and then, as soon as possible, have you trying things out for yourself. It's one thing to read about a process, but until you experience it for yourself it somehow isn't real!

During the many years in which I've been a technical writer I've encountered hundreds of handbooks for musical instruments, studio equipment, computers and software, and it still astounds me how badly some of them are organised. All too often they jump straight in and hurl facts at you before they've even given you an overview of the equipment in question. The information is all there, but you are often given no indication as to why you might need it or how best to apply it. I find this approach as difficult to deal with as anyone else!

Philosophical studies have discovered that we all create our own personal models of the world that allow us to get on with life without actually understanding more than the tiniest fraction of what really makes the universe tick. My intent is to do the same for MIDI. There are many definitive works on MIDI, but this isn't one of them. The aim of this book is to help you become a MIDI user – quickly. If you want to become a computer expert or a self-absorbed MIDI anorak, there are plenty of other books that will be able to help you.

why MIDI?

Before even attempting to explain MIDI, it's a good idea to have a look at what sort of things we might want to do with it. Indeed, you might even ask why we need it at all.

If you are an accomplished piano player who has no interest in recording or multi-part composition, it's probably fairly safe to say that MIDI is unlikely to play a major part in your life. Even so, don't close the book on MIDI just yet because there are some sequencers on the market with very advanced score-writing facilities which you might find useful. On the other hand, if you play an electronic keyboard and would like to put together multipart compositions featuring the sounds of a number of different instruments, complete with drums and percussion (all without involving other musicians), then MIDI sequencing is ideal for you.

MIDI isn't only applicable to keyboard players but, because the keyboard is the best-suited tool for generating MIDI information, the majority of MIDI music is made using them. However, there are practical alternatives for musicians who prefer to pluck, bow, blow or hit things, and these will be covered in the chapter on 'Methods Of Synthesis'.

a virtual orchestra

MIDI enables you to record all of the various musical parts of a score from a keyboard, one at a time, and then hear them playing together perfectly synchronised, each note reproduced with the synth sound of your choice. Also, consider the benefits of being able to change the sounds after you've finished recording, which even the simplest MIDI sequencing system will allow you to do. When using MIDI you have your own virtual orchestra at your fingertips. You can change the tempo of your finished recording without affecting the pitch, you can transpose the piece without affecting the tempo, and you can experiment with musical arrangements by cutting and pasting verses and choruses to new locations within the song.

The information that is communicated to a synthesiser from a sequencer via MIDI is exactly the same as that exchanged by a composer and a performer, except that the medium is computer memory and floppy disks and not a written score, and the instruments are electronic rather than acoustic.

the MIDI sequencer

In its most rudimentary application, MIDI means that a keyboard player can play several electronic instruments from a single keyboard rather than having to dash around the stage whenever a change of instrument is required. However, shortly after the introduction of MIDI came the MIDI sequencer, a special type of multitrack recorder capable of recording not sound but MIDI information. Before elaborating on this, I will first have to explain a few basic facts about what MIDI does and does not do. For example, it is important to bear in mind that MIDI doesn't make sounds: it controls sounds made by other equipment – in this case, your synthesiser.

I'd also like to assure you that, contrary to what some people would have you believe, MIDI is not something that 'takes over' your music or makes your work sound mechanical; it's simply a tool to do a job, and, like any tools, it can be used well or it can be used badly.

the keyboard

Whatever the nature of the MIDI system you decide to use, you will need a MIDI keyboard. Fortunately, these need not be expensive. If your keyboard has MIDI In, Out and Thru sockets on the back panel it's a MIDI keyboard. Even if you decide to use an alternative controller, such as a MIDI guitar system, you'll probably still find a keyboard useful. If possible, try and obtain a keyboard that has velocity sensitivity because this will respond like an authentic instrument in that the volume of the individual notes can be controlled by the amount of pressure exerted on the keys. If you don't have velocity sensitivity, all of the notes will sound at the same volume.

You can choose a dumb master keyboard with no built-in sounds or, instead, you can use a conventional keyboard synthesiser with its own store of voices as your master keyboard. Either will work perfectly well, so the choice is entirely up to you. However, if you choose a keyboard synth for use with a sequencer, it's important that it has a MIDI Local Off facility. The reasons for this will be explained later, but for now don't rush out and buy a synth if you're not sure that you can switch it to Local Off mode.

what is MIDI?

On the outside MIDI is simply a neat cable connecting two pieces of equipment, but inside it's a complicated digital data transmission system that requires quite a lot of specialised computer knowledge to fully understand. Thankfully it is not necessary for the musician to understand the inner workings of MIDI, in the same way that the workings of an international telephone exchange can be safely ignored by someone trying to phone their grandmother in Texas. In other words, the knowledge required to make use of MIDI bears almost no relationship to the complexity of the underlying technology. Indeed, most of the confusion surrounding MIDI seems to have stemmed from books that try to explain its inner workings in far too much depth.

the MIDI link

The linking of MIDI instruments is accomplished with standard MIDI cables, which are twin cored screened cables with five-pin DIN plugs on either end. And again, if you don't know what a DIN plug is, or if you have no desire to explore the inner world of twin-cored screened cables, it doesn't matter. If you go to the music shop and ask for a MIDI cable, the only technical parameter you need to know is how long you'd like it!

As mentioned previously, MIDI is a standard communication system that enables MIDI-equipped electronic instruments to be linked together regardless of the instruments' model or manufacturer. Like computers, the data is in digital form (a sort of ultra-fast Morse code for machines). The method of connecting MIDI instruments is quite straightforward, but it is important at this stage to appreciate precisely what musically useful information can be passed from one MIDI instrument or device to another.

The following basic description covers the most important aspects of MIDI. However, it is by no means comprehensive, and new concepts will be introduced only when they are needed. For now, information will be handed out on a strictly need-to-know basis. There are many excellent books which delve into the more frightening complexities of MIDI, and if after reading this book you feel better prepared to tackle them, this book will have served its purpose.

anatomy of a note

An electronic keyboard instrument is not like an acoustic piano, in which sound is created by a physical hammer hitting a string, causing it to vibrate at a certain pitch. Inside a keyboard the action of pressing a key generates electronic messages which tell the internal circuitry what note to play and how loud to play it. When a key is depressed on a MIDI keyboard, a signal known as a Note On message is sent from the MIDI Out socket, along with a note number identifying the key; when the key is released, a Note Off message is sent. This is the manner by which the receiving MIDI instrument knows which note to play, when to play it and when to stop playing it.

Up to 128 notes can be handled by MIDI, with each key on the keyboard being identified by its own note number.

The volume of the note depends on how hard the key is hit, which is really the same thing as saying how fast the key is pushed down. This speed, or velocity, is communicated by the Note On signal, read by circuitry within the keyboard and used to control the volume of the sound being played. The term velocity is one piece of MIDI jargon that will keep cropping up in this context, so it's a good idea to remember it.

The pitch of a note is usually determined by the key which is pressed. However, it is quite possible to transpose MIDI data before it reaches its destination, and so playing middle C doesn't necessarily result in that note being produced by the instrument. For the moment, however, let's keep things simple and assume that, unless otherwise stated, pressing a certain key results in the playing of its corresponding note.

MIDI note data

If pitch, Note On, Note Off and velocity information is communicated in the form of electronic signals, it therefore follows that it is also possible to send them along wires to control a MIDI instrument some distance away from the keyboard. A small computer inside the keyboard monitors the physical motion of the keys and converts these to MIDI messages, which appear at the MIDI Out socket of the keyboard. If we plug the MIDI Out of the keyboard we are playing (the master) into the MIDI In socket of a second MIDI instrument (the slave), the second instrument is then able to play the notes as performed on the master keyboard. This simple connection is shown in Figure 1.1, but don't try it just yet as there are one or two things that should be learnt first. For now, a brief description of the three terms used in MIDI connections are explained below (a complete glossary appears at the end of this book).

MIDI Out: sends information from a controlling device (master) to other MIDI devices that it is controlling (slaves).

MIDI In: receives MIDI information which is then passed on to the MIDI Thru socket unchanged. However, if any of the incoming information is 'addressed' to the instrument in question, it will act on that MIDI data exactly as if it were being controlled directly from a keyboard.

MIDI Thru: sends a copy of the MIDI In signal allowing several MIDI instruments to be linked together.

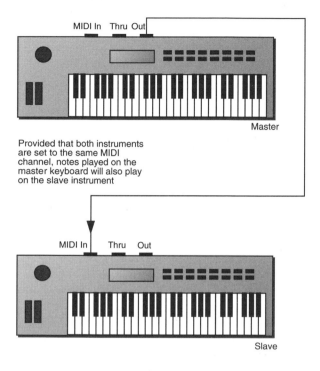

Figure 1.1: Basic MIDI connection (master/slave)

instructions, not sounds

Before moving on, it's worth repeating that MIDI isn't about transmitting sounds, it's about transmitting information that tells the instrument what you were playing on the master keyboard. It's surprising how many people listen patiently to a description of MIDI sequencing and then ask if they can record their voice over MIDI as well! Think of it like an automatic player-piano with a paper roll, where the roll is the recorded sequence and the piano itself is the sound module. There are ways of recording conventional audio sounds into certain computer-based MIDI sequencers, but that part of their operation has nothing at all to do with MIDI.

the keyboardless synthesiser

The ability to link a second instrument via MIDI means that the sounds of both instruments can be played by using just one keyboard. Of course, while this may be convenient it's hardly likely to revolutionise music as we know it. However, it's also apparent that the second instrument doesn't actually need a keyboard at all, as all of the physical manipulation of keys is performed on the master keyboard.

This leads nicely onto what is known as the MIDI module, which is simply the sound-generating and

MIDI-interfacing electronics of a keyboard instrument with the actual keyboard stripped away and with the electronic components packaged in a rather more compact and generally less expensive box. MIDI modules are much cheaper to build than fully-sized keyboard instruments and they also take up a lot less space (the electronics for a typical synthesiser module will fit into a box little larger than a chocolate box). It is also possible to control multiple modules from a single master keyboard, although to appreciate the full implications of this we must first investigate the concept of MIDI channels, the means by which certain messages are addressed in such a way that they are recognised by specific instruments and ignored by others.

MIDI channels

In a typical master/slave MIDI system the instruments are linked together like a daisy chain, and therefore they all receive the same MIDI information. The MIDI channel system was devised in order to allow the master instrument to communicate with just one specific slave, without all of the others trying to play along. The basic idea is that MIDI Note messages are tagged with an invisible address label carrying their MIDI channel number. In this way the messages are only acted upon when they are received by a MIDI instrument or device set to the same MIDI channel number. All other MIDI devices will politely ignore the message. The following analogy may make this clearer.

There are 16 MIDI channels which are, logically enough, numbered one to 16, and they are similar in nature to television channels. With TV transmissions, many different broadcasts arrive at the same socket and reach the TV set via the same piece of wire, but we can only watch one channel at a time. The signal we actually watch depends on the TV channel we select on the set. The key point here is that all of the programmes are fed into the TV set simultaneously, but the system of selecting channels allows us to tune into them one at a time.

It's exactly the same with MIDI. The information sent down the MIDI lead can be carried by any one of 16 channels as selected on the master keyboard. Likewise, the connected instruments may also be set to receive on any of the 16 channels, so if we set the master keyboard to MIDI channel one, for example, and connect three different MIDI instruments set to receive on channels one, two and three, only the instrument set to channel one will respond. The other instruments still receive the information, but the MIDI data tells them that the information is not on their channel so they simply ignore it. This arrangement is illustrated in Figure 1.2. By switching channels on the master keyboard, up to 16 different MIDI instruments set to 16 different channels can be addressed individually, even though they are all wired into the same system. It is vitally important to understand the MIDI channel system in order to understand MIDI sequencers.

If you feel like trying the example in Figure 1.1 now, go ahead – just make sure that both devices are set to the same MIDI channel. Most instruments arc sct to MIDI channel one, though this can be changed if necessary (instructions to this effect are usually printed in an instrument's operating manual).

omni mode warning

This next piece of information is covered in greater detail later in this book, but I'm mentioning it now because, if a MIDI instrument is inadvertently set to Omni mode (an option usually buried in the MIDI setup menu), the system won't behave as you'd expect. As well as receiving information on each of 16 channels, MIDI instruments can also be set to Omni mode, which will allow them to respond to all incoming data regardless of the channel via which it is

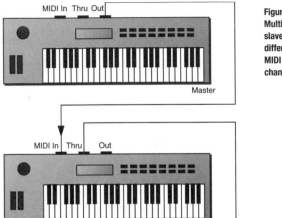

Figure 1.2:
Multiple
slaves on
different
MIDI
channels

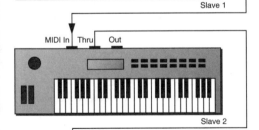

Slaves will only respond if they are on the same MIDI channel as the master. Note that all of the slaves are shown as keyboard instruments, whereas in practice it is more likely that some or all of them will be MIDI modules

sent. In other words, everything that comes along the MIDI cable is played, which is rather like having one member of an orchestra trying to play all parts of the score at the same time.

Some MIDI equipment, especially older models, tends to default to Omni mode when switched on, which means that the correct channel must then be set before any work can be done. Fortunately, the vast majority of instruments remember their MIDI configuration, even if they've been switched off. For normal 16-channel operation, instruments should be set to Poly mode. These modes will be explained in greater detail later.

more about modules

This book describes the basic workings of MIDI synthesisers and other MIDI instruments, but there are some aspects of MIDI synthesiser modules that need to be dealt with now so that what follows makes sense. So far I've described modules as MIDI synthesisers in boxes but without any keyboard, and as far as it goes this definition is true enough. However, many modern modules actually contain several independent sound-generating sections, each of which can be addressed on a different MIDI channel.

These sound-generating sections are often known as parts, because in a typical system each section can be assigned to play a separate musical part. For example, a 16-part multitimbral module can play back up to 16 different musical sounds at the same time, each controlled via a different MIDI channel. For most purposes it is possible to visualise a multipart module as being analogous to several synthesisers sharing the same box. Most computer soundcards also feature a MIDI synth section.

multitimbrality

Such multipart modules are said to be multitimbral, though the individual synthesiser sections contained within them are rarely entirely independent of each other. For example, they all share the same set of front-panel controls, and some parameters may globally affect all of the voices. What's more, on low-cost modules and soundcards the outputs from the various parts are usually mixed to stereo, and this signal then emerges via a single stereo pair of sockets. However, you'll invariably find that you have independent control over which of the available sounds (or patches, as they are referred to by professionals) are selected, along with the relative levels of the different voices, the pan positions and the amount of effect added to each part.

Samplers also tend to be multitimbral, but at this point they can be considered to be simply a specialised type of synthesiser. The section on the MIDI instruments provides an overview of samplers and their use.

Drum machines may also be considered to be MIDI modules, although they are equipped with internal sequencers which allow them to store and replay rhythm patterns and complex arrangements comprising numerous rhythm patterns. Most drum machines are not multitimbral – they can only play one part at a time, even though it may comprise a number of different drum sounds. If it proves necessary to control their sounds from a keyboard or via an external MIDI sequencer, it is possible to access their sounds externally over MIDI.

There is one fundamental difference between the ways in which a standard synth patch and a drum machine organise their sounds: a synthesiser usually interprets incoming MIDI note data as different pitches of the same basic sound, whereas a drum machine produces a different drum, cymbal or percussion sound for each MIDI note. Most multitimbral synthesiser modules and computer soundcards have one part of their circuitry dedicated to drum sounds, so it is no longer essential to buy a separate drum machine. The section on MIDI instruments includes more details concerning this.

MIDI sockets

On the back of a typical MIDI keyboard, instrument or sound module are three MIDI sockets labelled MIDI In, MIDI Thru and MIDI Out, although some models may not have all three, and Out and Thru are sometimes combined. It's now time to find out what these are for.

The master instrument in a simple MIDI chain sends information from its MIDI Out socket, which must be connected to the MIDI In socket of the first slave. The MIDI Thru of the first slave is then connected to the MIDI In of the second slave, and its Thru is then connected to the MIDI In of the next one in the series and so on. The resulting succession of connections resembles a daisy chain, and while in theory this can be indefinitely long this turns out to be untrue in practice. As it passes through each instrument the MIDI signal deteriorates slightly, and after it has gone through three or four instruments it starts to become unreliable and soon notes are getting stuck or they don't play at all. It's rather like the old game of Chinese whispers, with a group of people trying to pass a message along a line to hear how much it has changed when it arrives at the other end.

One solution is to use a MIDI Thru box. This device takes the MIDI Out signal from the master keyboard and then splits it into several Thru connections which feed the individual modules directly. Figure 1.2 describes the standard method of arranging daisy-chain connections, and Figure 1.3 shows the same connections wired using a MIDI Thru box. A MIDI Thru box is a relatively simple and inexpensive device which takes one MIDI input and provides two or more outputs carrying identical signals to the MIDI input data. In effect, it splits a single MIDI signal several ways. Thru boxes may also be used in combination with daisy chaining: if an instrument is fed from a Thru box, its Thru socket may be linked to another module to form a short daisy chain, the only proviso being that these individual chains are no more than one or two devices long.

Some people believe that chaining MIDI Thru connectors causes delays in timing, but this is simply not true. Most MIDI delays can be attributed to either too much data being sent at the same time or to delays incurred within the instruments themselves. For example, some synthesisers take several milliseconds to respond once a MIDI note message has been received.

programs and patches

We've established that MIDI operates on 16 channels and can be used to send information concerning note number, timing and velocity from a MIDI-compatible

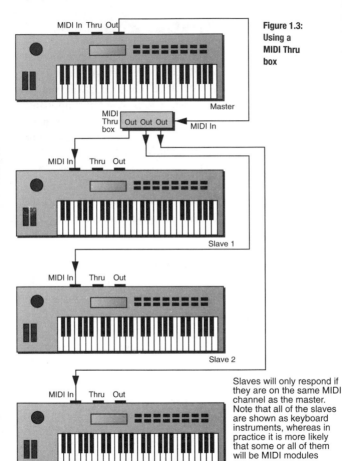

Figure 1.3: Using a MIDI Thru box

Slaves will only respond if they are on the same MIDI channel as the master. Note that all of the slaves are shown as keyboard instruments, whereas in practice it is more likely that some or all of them will be MIDI modules

master instrument to a MIDI-compatible slave. However, there is a great deal more information that also goes down the wire.

In the main, modern synthesisers are programmable, which means they have the ability to remember many different sounds, each identified by its patch or program number (these two terms being generally interchangeable). New instruments inevitably come with some preset factory patches (which can't be changed), along with room for users to store their own patches. Depending on the model of instrument, these user patches may be filled with sounds that can then be edited at will, or they may be empty. The term 'patch' is a throwback to very early electronic synthesisers, which used patch cables, rather like an old-fashioned telephone exchange, to connect the various sound-generating components.

MIDI can directly access up to 128 patches, sometimes numbered from 0 to 127 and sometimes from 1 to 128 (even standards aren't always all that standard!). The buttons that are used to select the patches on the master keyboard also enable patch information to be transmitted to the slave synthesiser modules, so now it is possible not only to play the modules remotely but also to select the sound or patch to which they are set.

These patch change commands are known as Program Change messages, and their use isn't limited to MIDI instruments – they may also be used to call up effects patches on MIDI-compatible effects units. If you have two MIDI instruments linked up so that the slave can be played from the master, try pressing the Program Change buttons on the master. You should find that the slave also changes to the new patch number.

Because MIDI Program Change messages can only access 128 patches directly, instruments containing more than 128 patches must have these organised into two or more banks, each containing a maximum of 128 patches per bank. Bank Change commands, comprising specific MIDI controller data, are used to switch from one bank to the next. More of that later.

Some studio effects units are MIDI controllable, and MIDI program changes can be used to call up specific effects from a library of different effects patches. However, MIDI Program Change messages are just one aspect of what MIDI is capable; there's an awful lot more useful information that can travel down that cable. MIDI also serves a secondary purpose in allowing synchronisation signals to be sent between devices such as drum machines and sequencers, and there's a section devoted to this subject later in this book.

controlling MIDI

Real musical instruments aren't just concerned with pitches and volume: they're also about expression. A violin player, for example, may add vibrato to a note or slide from one note to another. To help the keyboard player imitate the expression of a real instrument, a typical MIDI synthesiser or master keyboard has two or more performance wheels mounted to the left of the keyboard, one of which is usually dedicated to pitch bend. The other wheel, or wheels, can sometimes be reassigned to allow them to control various different effects, though the most common application is to control depth of vibrato. Like the keys, these controllers work by generating electronic signals which, in turn, control the circuitry that creates the sound. And like note information, this control information may also be sent over MIDI – move the control wheel on the master and the slave will respond.

Further control may be provided by means of foot switches or pedal inputs, which will allow a conventional volume pedal to be used as a means of varying MIDI control functions, such as the level of filter frequency.

Because pedals and wheels can be set to any one of a number of different positions, and are not restricted to simply being on or off, they are known as continuous controllers. In everyday terms, a car's steering wheel and accelerator can be thought of as being continuous controllers, whereas the direction indicators are simple switched controllers that are either on or off.

However, continuous controllers aren't as continuous as they might seem. MIDI deals with numbers, and because of the data structure used to effect these changes the available range is still restricted from 0 to 127. This means that all continuous controllers really operate over a series of tiny steps, but as the steps are small enough to be indiscernible the effect is that of a smooth gradation.

The different devices by which a musical instrument may be controlled include performance wheels, joysticks, levers, pedals, foot switches, breath controllers, ribbon controllers and other less obvious but equally ingenious devices. All can be employed to exert their influence via MIDI controllers, which is why using MIDI allows so many different controllers to be used at the same time. You don't have to worry about MIDI channels or other technicalities when using controllers, as all of the data is automatically fed to the same destination (MIDI channel) as the notes played on the keyboard.

In order to obtain more precision than that which can be afforded by 128 steps, two controllers must be used simultaneously. For this purpose, the MIDI specification reserves a number of controllers. However, this degree of precision is rarely necessary or desirable, as an increase in the amount of MIDI data generated will likewise increase the chances of a MIDI data traffic jam.

pitch-bend scaling

By changing parameters in the MIDI setup section, MIDI instruments can often be scaled so that, for example, moving the pitch bend wheel to its upper or lower limit might cause a pitch shift of as little as one semitone or as much as a whole octave. As you can imagine, it is important to ensure that any instruments likely to play at the same time are set with the same scaling values, especially for pitch bend. Otherwise, when a note is pressed on the master keyboard, the sound coming from the master instrument might go up by four semitones and the sound from the slave by five, which is clearly not desirable unless you're hoping to invent a new strain of modern jazz! For general use, most people set up a pitch-bend range of two semitones so that a range of plus or minus one whole tone is available by moving the wheel from its centre position to its upper or lower limit. Most pitch-bend wheels are spring loaded so that they automatically return to their neutral position when released. Interestingly, although the pitch wheel is involved in controlling expression, it doesn't form a part of the group of MIDI controllers but instead exists in a category of its own. This is almost certainly due to reasons firmly rooted in tradition.

more controllers

Another important controller is master volume. Some instruments send and respond to it and some don't. On an instrument that does, turning up the slider which controls the master volume will send the appropriate control information (controller seven) over the MIDI interface and the receiving synth will respond to it. A multitimbral module receiving a master volume control message will vary the volume of whichever part is being addressed according to the MIDI channel of the message. Be warned, however, that some older instruments don't respond to controller seven, so any attempts to control the volume of these instruments via MIDI will prove fruitless.

Another commonly-used MIDI controller is the sustain pedal, which prevents note envelopes from entering their release phase until the pedal is released. The MIDI sustain pedal operates just like the sustain pedal on the piano.

The MIDI spec is constantly evolving, and not all 128 possible controller numbers are used – yet! Controllers 0 to 63 are used for continuous controllers while 64 to 95 are used for switches. 96 to 121 are undefined and 122 to 127 are reserved for Channel Mode messages. A full listing of the Controller numbers and their functions follows, but don't panic if some of them don't make any sense at the moment.

controller listing

0	Bank Select
1	Modulation Wheel
2	Breath Controller
3	Undefined
4	Foot Controller

5	Portamento Time
6	Data Entry
7	Main Volume
8	Balance
9	Undefined
10	Pan
11	Expression
12	Effect Control 1
13	Effect Control 2
14	Undefined
15	Undefined
16-19	General Purpose 1-4
20-31	Undefined
32-63	LSB for Control Changes 0-31 (where greater resolution is required)
64	Damper/Sustain Pedal
65	Portamento
66	Sostenuto
67	Soft Pedal
68	Legato Footswitch
69	Hold 2
70	Sound Variation/Exciter
71	Harmonic Content/Compressor
72	Release Time/Distortion
73	Attack Time/Equaliser
74	Brightness/Expander (Gate)
75	Undefined/Reverb

76	Undefined/Delay
77	Undefined/Pitch Transpose
78	Undefined/Flange-Chorus
79	Undefined/Special Effect
80-83	General Purpose 5-8
84	Portamento Control
85-90	Undefined
91	Effect Depth (Effect 1)
92	Tremolo Depth (Effect 2)
93	Chorus Depth (Effect 3)
94	Celeste Depth (Effect 4)
95	Phaser Depth (Effect 5)
96	Data Increment
97	Data Decrement
98	Non-Registered Parameter Number LSB
99	Non-Registered Parameter Number MSB
100	Registered Parameter Number LSB
101	Registered Parameter Number MSB
102-119	Undefined
120	All Sound Off
121	Reset All Controllers
122	Local Control
123	All Notes Off
124	Omni Mode Off
125	Omni Mode On
126	Mono Mode On
127	Poly Mode On

As you can see, not all controllers deal with performance control. The last four controller numbers toggle MIDI modes, and as well as these there are also Bank Change messages, an All Notes Off message (to cut off all notes that may still be playing), Local On/Off and a Reset All Controllers message, so that all controller values can be reset to their default values. Most of these will have little impact on your day-to-day use of MIDI, although those instances where they are useful will be discussed later. Most of the time, at least while you're getting to know MIDI, you'll be concerned mainly with selecting and playing sounds, with using the performance wheels on the master keyboard and possibly with the sustain pedal, which is also plugged into the master keyboard.

MSB and LSB stand for Most Significant and Least Significant Byte – roughly speaking, computer terminology for coarse and fine adjustments. Both MSBs and LSBs have a possible numerical range of 0 to 127, so no surprises there! In fact, all variable controllers have values of between 0 and 127, while switched controllers are usually set at 0 for off and 127 for on. Most modern instruments will also accept any value of 64 and above as on and any value below 64 as off, though some older instruments are more choosy.

Pitch bend can provide control in two directions, so its default position is midway between the two extremes: 64. Again, you don't need to dive into the guts of MIDI at this stage, as your sequencer will take care of most of the obscure MIDI dialogue to and from your keyboard and modules for you. However, when you come to edit MIDI sequence data it is helpful to know what the more common controllers and their values mean.

non-registered parameters

Because not all synthesisers use the same type of synthesis, it would be impossible to provide a standard range of controllers able to access every parameter that had an influence over the sound being produced. Some parameters are common to all instruments, and these are known as registered parameters, but to allow manufacturers to provide access to all the relevant parameters of different instruments, the non-registered parameter (NRPN) system was added to the MIDI specification.

The registered parameters are pitch-bend sensitivity, fine tuning, coarse tuning, change tuning program and change tuning bank. The vast majority of controls are non-registered, however, although for precisely that reason some form of customised hardware interface or editing software is usually needed to access them. Because they are non-defined, the typical user has no means of knowing what they are unless they are listed in the MIDI spec at the back of the instrument's manual. However, NRPNs provide a convenient back door through which designers and software writers can access the invisible sound-control elements inside synthesisers without having to get involved in the complexities of system-exclusive messages.

channel voice messages

Most MIDI messages are channel specific, in that they are only accepted by the receiving device if that device is set to the same channel on which the data is being sent. MIDI Note Ons and Offs are channel messages, as are all other types of performance data relating to velocity, pitch bend, controller data, program changes and so on.

A single musical note can be represented by a fairly concise MIDI message comprising only a channel number, a Note On event followed by a Note Off event, and a velocity value. Controller information, on the other hand, is rather more data intensive because, as long as you're moving a controller, it is sending out a continuous stream of MIDI data.

aftertouch

Another source of musical performance control information is channel aftertouch, which is produced by some keyboards when the keys are pressed hard. This works by means of a pressure sensor located under the keyboard which sends out lots of MIDI data, whether the receiving device responds to it or not. Therefore, if you're not using the aftertouch on your master keyboard, turning it off will prevent the system from becoming clogged up with unnecessary data. I tend to leave it off as a matter of course unless I specifically need it, because when you're working with a computer sequencer unnecessary controller data takes up a lot of memory.

Aftertouch can be assigned to various functions, such as brightness, loudness, depth of vibrato and so on. It is a useful way of adding expression to a performance, but you should keep in mind that channel aftertouch affects all of the notes that are currently playing, not just the one you're pressing down on.

A few exotic instruments also feature polyphonic aftertouch, which means that, when a key is pressed down, the data sent applies only to that note and not to all of the notes that are currently playing. Polyphonic aftertouch can generate a vast amount of MIDI data and so it must be used sparingly, and only very few instruments support this facility.

Release velocity is another very rare feature. All touch-velocity instruments generate MIDI note velocity, depending on how quickly the keys are pushed down, but an instrument with release velocity will generate additional information depending on how quickly the keys are released.

sound banks

As discussed earlier, the maximum range of a conventional MIDI message is from 0 to 127, which means that MIDI can address a maximum of 128 different notes or send controller information with a maximum of 128 discrete values. Similarly, it is only possible to directly address 128 different patches. However, to get around this limitation some synths organise their sounds into multiple banks, each with a maximum of 128 patches per bank. MIDI Bank Change messages (which are also forms of controller message, involving the controller numbers 0 and 32) are then used to access the different banks. Not all Bank Change messages are standard, but the relevant controller values will be supplied in your MIDI instrument's handbook as part of the MIDI implementation table. Some of the more modern sequencers include a library of Bank Change commands for the more common instruments in circulation, so once you've told your sequencer to which instrument it's connected it will automatically send the right Bank Change command.

assignable controls

Instruments often allow you to determine which physical control device relates to a specific MIDI controller, which means that the modulation wheel on your synth could be redirected to control something quite different, such as amount of reverb or the brightness of the sound being played.

How much you want to get involved with the various controllers is up to you. At first you'll probably be quite happy to restrict yourself with the pitch bend and modulation wheels and the sustain pedal, but as you become more familiar with MIDI you may become attracted to the possibilities of using a sequencer to automate your performance by controlling levels, creating automated panning, changing effects and patch changes, and so on. The great thing about MIDI is that you can start off very simply, making music right from the outset, and then, as you become more comfortable with the concept, you can try to be more ambitious. Also, most modern sequencers provide graphically-driven ways of editing and using controller data, and so you can probably achieve most of what you want to without ever getting bogged down in the technical details.

MIDI clock

Unlike channel-specific messages, MIDI messages related to synchronisation and sequencer control have no channel address, and so these are received by all of the instruments in the MIDI system. Perhaps the most important of all these messages is MIDI clock.

MIDI clock is a tempo-related timing code comprising 96 electronic 'clocks', or ticks, for each four-beat bar of music. Think of it as the invisible conductor that keeps your drum machine and sequencer or your sequencer and tape recorder playing together rather than going their own separate ways. You can't hear these ticks, but they are picked up by any drum machine or sequencer set to External MIDI Sync mode, enabling the slave machine to stay in sync with the master.

A practical use of MIDI clock is to sync up a drum

machine to a sequencer so that either can be the master. Using a suitable interface box, it's also possible to use MIDI clock to keep a sequencer running in time with a recording on tape. The slave machine must be set to External MIDI Sync mode, which means that it will follow exactly the tempo generated by the master device.

start, stop and continue

The slave device also needs to know when to start and stop, so MIDI also includes messages to tell the device to start, stop and continue. Even so, these are only of any use if you start your master from the beginning of the song, or the slave won't know from where it's supposed to start. To solve this problem, the MIDI Song Position Pointer message was added to the MIDI specification. This is quite obvious to the user, but on starting the sequence a message is sent which tells the receiving device where to start from. As a result, the slave device can lock up almost instantaneously. So-called Smart FSK (Frequency Shift Keying) tape-to-MIDI sync boxes using MIDI song position pointers are often used to make a MIDI sequencer synchronise to a tape machine. A full section is dedicated to issues concerning MIDI synchronisation later in the book.

There is also a protocol for controlling compatible tape machines and hard disk recorders, which is known as MIDI Machine Control (MMC). This allows remote access to the main transport controls and record status buttons of a multitrack recorder, which can prove useful if your multitrack recorder is at the opposite side of the room from your sequencer.

MIDI overcrowding

While I've promised to try to keep this book as non-technical as possible, it helps in understanding the limitations of MIDI to know that it is a serial system – in other words, information moves in single file. At this point, many books on MIDI present you with an in-depth description of the bits and bytes that make up a MIDI message, and if you're technically minded this can be quite interesting. However, as this doesn't really enable the typical user to make better use of MIDI I make no apology for omitting it entirely.

The main point is that, because MIDI is relatively fast, things may seem to happen all at once, but in reality, when a chord is played the notes start to sound one after the other, not simultaneously. This delay between each note is far too short to be perceptible when only a few events are concerned, but if you were to try to play

64 notes at once, for example, you might just hear a delay between the first and the last.

In reality, the speed of MIDI is seldom a limitation when you're dealing with only notes, but if you're trying to replay a multipart MIDI sequence that also contains lots of controller information you could end up with the MIDI equivalent of a traffic jam, resulting in timing errors. In practice it's wise to use controllers only when necessary, and to switch off your master keyboard's aftertouch whenever you don't need it. The better-quality sequencers give priority to MIDI note timing when traffic gets heavy so that timing problems are less likely to be audible.

MIDI modes

Instruments are generally set to Poly mode for conventional operation, though some older instruments default to Omni mode every time they are switched on. Because the vast majority of work is carried out in Poly mode, most users rarely give MIDI modes a second thought. However, there are actually four different MIDI modes:

Mode 1: Omni On/Poly. The instrument will play polyphonically but MIDI channel data is ignored.

Whatever you send it, on whatever channel, will be played. Some older instruments still default to Omni mode when they're powered up so they need to be switched back to Omni Off mode before use.

Mode 2: Omni On/Mono. The monophonic equivalent of Mode 1 – hardly ever used.

Mode 3: Omni Off/Poly. The 'normal' MIDI mode, used especially for sequencing or multitimbral operation. In Mode 3, the instrument responds to messages on its own MIDI channel only and plays polyphonically.

Mode 4: Omni Off/Mono. The monophonic equivalent of Mode 3. Mode 4 is mainly used by MIDI guitar players who need to have each string working on a separate MIDI channel in order to be able to bend notes or apply vibrato on independent strings. Because each string of a guitar is mono (it can only play one note at a time) it makes sense to use the receiving synth in mono mode to mimic the way a real guitar is played.

active sensing

MIDI also includes something called active sensing, which (while not always implemented) is MIDI's way of checking that a connection exists between devices. In reality, it's the MIDI equivalent of the receiving device shouting 'Are you still there?' If, after a short while, the transmitting device doesn't shout back 'Yes!', the receiving device assumes that the transmitting device has gone off-line.

What really happens is that, if the receiving device isn't sent an 'all's well' message within the allowed time, it shuts off all of those notes that are being played. If it didn't, and the MIDI cable was accidentally unplugged between a Note On being sent and a Note Off being sent, the receiving instrument would continue to play that note until it eventually rusted away! Happily, this too is completely hidden from the user, but it's nice to know that it's there. It's also easy to determine if your system has active sensing: just unplug the MIDI cable while some notes are being played (while the keys are held down) and then wait to see if the noise stops. If it does then you have active sensing.

song select

Because MIDI sequencers can hold more than one song in their memory, MIDI also includes a Song Select message. As you might expect, tunes can be requested by number in the range 0 to 127. Think of it as a MIDI jukebox that accepts requests via Song Select numbers!

We're very used to MIDI instruments being perfectly in tune, but it is still possible for MIDI-controlled analogue synths to drift in pitch over a period of time unless they have intelligent auto-retuning systems. However, many of them have an internal tuning routine which can be initiated manually or over MIDI by using a Tune Request command. If such a command is sent, all of the MIDI instruments in the system that have a tuning routine will give themselves a quick diagnostic and retune to their own internal reference. With a little more MIDI experience, you may want to include this message in the count-in bars of your default song (a 'blank canvas' MIDI song that includes your special settings) so that your synth is automatically tuned up before the song starts. Check how long this takes, though, as you may need to add a few more count-in bars to make sure that the tuning routine is over before the music starts.

system-exclusive messages

'System exclusive' is a term that strikes terror into the hearts of those who know just enough about MIDI to know where the tricky bits are, but I mention it here so that, if you decide to ignore it, at least you'll know what you're ignoring!

System exclusive (or Sysex) messages are part of the MIDI system message portfolio, but whereas the rest of MIDI is defined fairly precisely Sysex is provided so that manufacturers can build instruments with different facilities yet which still conform to the MIDI specification. Rather than using the MIDI channel system for locating their targets, Sysex messages contain an identification code unique to the type of instrument for which they are intended. Whenever two or more identical instruments are being used in the same system, it's often possible to assign an additional ID number of between 1 and 16 to each so that no two have exactly the same ID. If they did, they'd all respond to the same Sysex data.

In the main, Sysex allows those clever people who write sound-editing software to gain access to all of those sound-generating parameters that might need adjusting. The programming parameters of analogue and digital synths are usually quite different, so if you want to provide access to these parameters via MIDI then manufacturers must be allowed to specify exclusive codes to access their specific set of parameters, just as they provide NRPNs to access certain unique parameters using MIDI controllers. This obviously couldn't be done using standardised codes, as every different make and model of synth has different parameters, and so Sysex was developed as a method of achieving this.

Because Sysex messages are only recognised by the type of instrument for which they are designed, there's no need to worry that your drum machine might try to interpret a message intended for one of your synths or vice versa. If the manufacturer's ID at the start of the Sysex message code isn't recognised by the receiving instrument then the message is ignored.

patch dumping

Usually, only experienced MIDI users have more than a passing association with MIDI Sysex data, but it's possible for anyone to use it at a basic level for copying patches or banks of patches from a synth into a MIDI storage device such as a sequencer or MIDI data filter. Here's how.

You'll find that most modern MIDI instruments have a Sysex dump facility tucked away in their MIDI configuration pages somewhere. All you have to do is connect the MIDI Out of the instrument in question to your sequencer's input, start the sequencer recording and then begin the dump procedure. The Sysex data will be recorded in exactly the same way as MIDI notes, although if you look in the edit list to see what's there you'll see nothing but nonsense. Nevertheless, the synth knows what it means, and that's all that matters.

Sysex dump data usually takes several seconds to record, after which it can be played back into the instrument at any time to restore the patches you saved. If you're in the habit of using lots of different patches in your songs and you don't have enough user memories to hold them all, you can store a Sysex dump right at the start of each song to set up the required patches for you. Depending on how long the dump takes, you may have to leave a few bars of count-in to allow it to finish before the music starts. Once you've loaded your new sounds it might be a good idea to mute the Sysex track, or the patches will be reloaded every time you start the song from the beginning. It's also important not to quantise the Sysex dump after recording, or it may not play back properly. If this last section doesn't make sense, read it again after you've read the chapter introducing sequencers. This is the trouble with MIDI – because of the way it evolved, it isn't always possible to keep everything in a perfectly logical order.

compatibility

If you expect every MIDI instrument to support every feature implemented in the MIDI specifications then you're destined to lead a sad and disappointed life. Most new instruments support most of the features but few are actually compulsory, and just about the only thing that can be taken for granted is that a MIDI synth will send and receive MIDI note data, though virtually all will accept MIDI program changes and velocity information. If a MIDI message is received by an instrument incapable of responding to that message then the message is simply ignored, in much the way as you might ignore junk mail written in a foreign language.

You should be aware, however, that different instruments can legitimately respond to the same MIDI message in different ways. To take previous example, the pitch-bend range of an instrument is not restricted to the data received but is pre-determined in the MIDI menu of the instrument itself. Therefore, full movement of the pitch-bend wheel (which equates to 128 tiny steps, with 64 denoting the middle position) can be calibrated to shift the pitch by as little as one semitone or by as much as an octave. Unless all of your instruments are set to the same pitch-bend range, you could end up with an horrendous discord. A pitch-bend range of two semitones is popular.

As I mentioned earlier in this chapter, very few instruments incorporate polyphonic key pressure (aftertouch) or release velocity, but just about every MIDI-compatible instrument you can buy now (other than some really basic home keyboards) is velocity sensitive, and even some relatively inexpensive keyboards have channel aftertouch. Some older instruments don't respond to MIDI Bank Change messages, even if they have banks of sounds which are accessible from the front panel. This can be incredibly frustrating. You may also come across some instruments which refuse to respond to controller seven (master volume) commands. If in doubt, you should be able to find a table of those MIDI facilities which are supported in the back of the relevant equipment manual, where 'O' shows that the facility is present and 'X' shows that it is not supported. This is known as a MIDI implementation table, and once you know what to look for you'll find that it can tell you a lot about the capabilities of your instrument in a very short space of time.

MIDI merge

If there is a need to split the same MIDI signal to two or more destinations, you can use either the Thru connectors fitted to the various MIDI instruments or a MIDI Thru box. That said, however, merging two streams of MIDI data isn't quite as simple. MIDI data is complex, so if you were to try to join two MIDI cables with a Y-lead the result would be a jumble of meaningless data. Figure 2.1 shows how a MIDI merge box might be used to merge the MIDI output from a keyboard and from a dedicated sound-editing device, enabling both signals to be fed into a sequencer at the same time.

To merge two or more MIDI data streams a specialised merge box is needed. These devices contain a small computer which is designed to interleave the data in a coherent way. Merge facilities are required in those cases when a sequencer needs to be controlled by a master keyboard at the same time as receiving MIDI sync signals, or when it becomes necessary to play two keyboards into your sequencer at the same time. There are other requirements for MIDI merge facilities which will be explained as they come up.

Although stand-alone MIDI merge boxes are now widely available on the market, some of the more sophisticated multiport MIDI interfaces include two or more mergeable inputs. By using a merge facility, it is also possible to have two or more MIDI keyboards

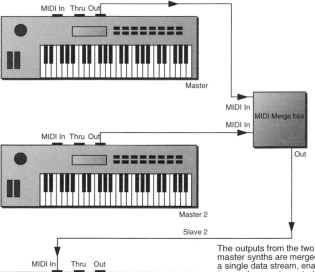

The outputs from the two master synths are merged into a single data stream, enabling two performers to control the same slave module simultaneously. A more realistic use is to allow two performers to record two parts into a sequencer at the same time, or to merge the output from a MIDI keyboard with an external MIDI controller, such as a pedal or breath controller

Figure 2.1: A MIDI Merge box in use

routed to the same system at once. This can often prove useful, for example when there are two players wishing to record different parts of a musical sequence at the same time.

chapter 3

general MIDI

Soundcards, along with general-purpose synths and modules, frequently include a set of General MIDI preset sounds, which is essentially a standard bank of 128 sounds that ensures nominal sound compatibility between instruments of different makes. Some GM synths sound better than others, but if you've created a composition for a piano at least you know it's going to play back with a piano sound, not a violin or a helicopter!

General MIDI was a relatively late addition to the MIDI spec, but it's extremely useful as it allows commercial MIDI files to be produced on those occasions when the writer can be pretty sure of what types of sounds are going to be used to play back his composition. The GM sound set includes a number of standard pop and classical sounds as well as synth sounds and sound effects, all located at the same patch numbers, regardless of the instrument or its manufacturer.

General MIDI is simply another stage of standardisation which has been added to the existing MIDI protocol. However, it doesn't have to be adopted by all MIDI instruments, only by those bearing the GM logo. Furthermore, a GM-compatible machine may also be able to function as a non-GM machine, in which case it will have a dedicated GM mode or separate bank of GM sounds for those occasions when General MIDI is required.

GM was developed to enable manufacturers to build synthesisers and synth modules that exhibited a specified degree of compatibility in terms of which sounds were located in which patches, to which keys the various drum sounds were mapped, and on the minimum performance capability of the machine in terms of multitimbrality and polyphony. Essentially, the aim is to allow a MIDI sequence recorded using one GM module to be played back on any other GM module without needing to remap patches, move drum-note allocations or worry about running out of parts or polyphony. This doesn't mean that all GM synths have to sound exactly the same, but it does mean that, for example, a piano preset on one machine must be in the same patch location as a similar-sounding piano preset on any other GM-compatible machine.

MIDI compatibility

Normally, whenever you record a piece of music using a sequencer, you insert the appropriate Program Change command at the start of each track so that, whenever the sequence is played back through the same instruments and modules, the correct sounds will automatically be called up. However, if you play the sequence back on a friend's non-GM system, you may well find that all of the sounds are completely wrong because the patches are not only completely different in sound but also because any that are suitable are probably stored in different patch locations. In the case of programmable instruments, this kind of chaos is difficult to avoid because most users have their own system for storing their edited sounds. Furthermore, the factory presets provided with non-GM instruments are usually arranged fairly arbitrarily. For this reason, it's useful to have at least one GM-compatible instrument in your collection so that you can play commercial GM-format MIDI files or sequences from musicians with whom you collaborate.

drum mapping

Another potential stumbling block is the part governing drums and percussion. Even if your friend's drum sounds are on the same MIDI channel as yours, the chances are that some or all of the drum sounds will be assigned to different keys. Roland have had their own more or less standard drum mapping system for some time now, but some other manufacturers have not been as well organised, so at the location you programmed a bass drum your friend's setup might play a cowbell. Furthermore, you may have written the piece using drum sounds that don't have any close equivalent on your friend's drum machine. The GM drum set at least ensures that all of the drum sounds are mapped to the same keys, and that a bass drum will always be a bass drum on each GM machine, even if doesn't sound exactly the same as the one you have at home.

polyphony and multitimbrality

The problem with polyphony and multitimbrality is that you can never have enough of it! General MIDI instruments provide the ability to play back 16 parts on 16 MIDI channels, with a total polyphony of at least 24 notes. In other words, there may be 16 different sounds running on 16 different MIDI channels, but the total number of notes playing at once can never exceed the maximum polyphony of the instrument.

If you try to play more notes than the instrument can handle you will experience note robbing, and previously-played notes will start to drop out. What's more, if a synth layers two voices to make up a sound the actual polyphony may be further reduced depending on how the manufacturer chooses to interpret the General MIDI spec on polyphony. The whole idea of specifying a minimum level of polyphony is so that you don't run out of it when trying to play a MIDI song file conforming to the GM format.

Roland's enhanced GS format

Much of the present GM format owes its existence to Roland's own protocols, so it's hardly surprising that Roland have gone one step further and devised an enhanced version of General MIDI which they call GS. Realising that many users wouldn't be satisfied with 128 preset GM sounds, Roland have designed their GS machines to offer several alternative banks of sounds, with the basic GM set (capital tones) designated as the first bank (bank zero). There are up to seven variation tones based on each of the capital tones, and these are arranged to have the same Program Change numbers as the tones from which they are derived. In other words, all of the variation tones of a piano capital tone will still be various piano voices, though they will all be subtly different. Further banks are provided for sounds known as sub-capital tones, which are less obviously related to the capital tones.

A Bank Change command allows the user to switch between the various banks. Conventional Program Change commands are then used to select the sounds within each bank, which is a neat way of getting around MIDI's limitation of being able to directly address only 128 patches. Yamaha also introduced their own expanded General MIDI format, which they call XG. Like Roland's GS mode, this enhances the basic General MIDI sound set with several banks of alternative sounds, but unfortunately a different Bank Change command is required to access these. At the time of writing, it seems that most Yamaha instruments also support Roland's GS format, so it looks as though GS will become the *de facto* standard for enhanced GM instruments.

editing

Because General MIDI is based on the concept of the same sounds always being in the same place, it stands to reason that any attempt at editing the sounds will negate any advantages the system has. Different instruments handle this dilemma in different ways, but as a rule you can switch between a GM mode based on preset sounds or a non-GM mode where editing is permitted.

commercial MIDI song files

Commercial GM song files are now available which cover all musical styles, from pop to classical, and these files have many applications, from general interest to song analysis. They are also used by solo performers to provide musical backings, within the conditions imposed by musical copyright law.

The huge advantage that MIDI song files have over pre-recorded backing tapes is that the key and/or tempo can be changed at the touch of a button, making life rather less difficult for the solo entertainer. The overall sound quality is generally better, too, as with pre-recorded tapes you either have to play the original night after night and risk wearing it out or copy it onto another cassette, which also degrades the quality of the sound.

aims of general MIDI

- A GM instrument must support all 16 MIDI channels simultaneously to provide 16-part multitimbrality.

- Percussion parts must be on MIDI channel ten, and a minimum set of 47 standard sound types, including the most common drum and Latin percussion sounds, must be provided. These must all be mapped in accordance with the GM standard. This mapping owes a lot to Roland's original mapping system.

- GM instruments must be capable of 24-note polyphony and notes must be allocated dynamically. However, the specification allows eight notes to be reserved for percussion, leaving 16 for the other instruments.

- All 128 preset sounds are defined in relation to their type and patch location. Though there is some variation in sound between one module and another, the instrument type (and even playing style, for example with basses) for each patch location is quite rigidly defined, right down to the dog barks, helicopters and gunshots in the special effects section. Some of the more abstract pad sounds are a little more flexible, but they must still be of a roughly similar tone and character.

- All GM instruments must respond to the same set of MIDI controllers, and the default ranges set for these controllers must be standard. The implementation of MIDI controllers includes the ability to change the master tuning and pitch-bend wheel range via MIDI, Reset All Controllers (which resets all MIDI controllers to their default values) and All Notes Off, which silences any notes currently playing. All GM machines must also respond to pitch bend, velocity and aftertouch.

GM voice table

Program No	Instrument	Program No	Instrument
1	Acoustic Grand Piano	19	Rock Organ
2	Bright Acoustic Piano	20	Church Organ
3	Electric Grand Piano	21	Reed Organ
4	Honky-Tonk Piano	22	Accordion
5	Electric Piano 1	23	Harmonica
6	Electric Piano 2	24	Tango Accordion
7	Harpsichord	25	Acoustic Guitar (Nylon)
8	Clavichord		
9	Celesta	26	Acoustic Guitar (Steel)
10	Glockenspiel		
11	Music Box	27	Electric Guitar (Jazz)
12	Vibraphone	28	Electric Guitar (Clean)
13	Marimba		
14	Xylophone	29	Electric Guitar (Muted)
15	Tubular Bells		
16	Dulcimer	30	Overdriven Guitar
17	Drawbar Organ	31	Distortion Guitar
18	Percussive Organ	32	Guitar Harmonics

Program No	Instrument	Program No	Instrument
33	Acoustic Bass	58	Trombone
34	Electric Bass (Finger)	59	Tuba
35	Electric Bass (Pick)	60	Muted Trumpet
36	Fretless Bass	61	French Horn
37	Slap Bass 1	62	Brass Section
38	Slap Bass 2	63	SynthBrass 1
39	Synth Bass 1	64	SynthBrass 2
40	Synth Bass 2	65	Soprano Sax
41	Violin	66	Alto Sax
42	Viola	67	Tenor Sax
43	Cello	68	Baritone Sax
44	Contrabass	69	Oboe
45	Tremolo Strings	70	English Horn
46	Pizzicato Strings	71	Bassoon
47	Orchestral Harp	72	Clarinet
48	Timpani	73	Piccolo
49	String Ensemble 1	74	Flute
50	String Ensemble 2	75	Recorder
51	Synth Strings 1	76	Pan Flute
52	Synth Strings 2	77	Blown Bottle
53	Choir Aahs	78	Shakuhachi
54	Voice Oohs	79	Whistle
55	Synth Voice	80	Ocarina
56	Orchestra Hit	81	Lead 1 (Square)
57	Trumpet	82	Lead 2 (Sawtooth)

Program No	Instrument	Program No	Instrument
83	Lead 3 (Calliope)	106	Banjo
84	Lead 4 (Chiff)	107	Shamisen
85	Lead 5 (Charang)	108	Koto
86	Lead 6 (Voice)	109	Kalimba
87	Lead 7 (Fifths)	110	Bagpipes
88	Lead 8 (Bass & Lead)	111	Fiddle
89	Pad 1 (New Age)	112	Shanai
90	Pad 2 (Warm)	113	Tinkle Bell
91	Pad 3 (Polysynth)	114	Agogo
92	Pad 4 (Choir)	115	Steel Drums
93	Pad 5 (Bowed)	116	Woodblock
94	Pad 6 (Metallic)	117	Taiko Drum
95	Pad 7 (Halo)	118	Melodic Tom
96	Pad 8 (Sweep)	119	Synth Drum
97	FX 1 (Rain)	120	Reverse Cymbal
98	FX 2 (Soundtrack)	121	Guitar Fret Noise
99	FX 3 (Crystal)	122	Breath Noise
100	FX 4 (Atmosphere)	123	Seashore
101	FX 5 (Brightness)	124	Bird Tweet
102	FX 6 (Goblins)	125	Telephone Ring
103	FX 7 (Echoes)	126	Helicopter
104	FX 8 (Sci-Fi)	127	Applause
105	Sitar	128	Gunshot

Note: some manufacturers number their patches from 0-127 rather than from 1-128

GM drum map

Note No	Drum Sound	Note No	Drum Sound
35	Acoustic Bass Drum	59	Ride Cymbal 2
36	Bass Drum 1	60	High Bongo
37	Side Stick	61	Low Bongo
38	Acoustic Snare	62	Mute Hi Conga
39	Hand Clap	63	Open Hi Conga
40	Electric Snare	64	Low Conga
41	Low Floor Tom	65	High Timbale
42	Closed Hi-Hat	66	Low Timbale
43	High Floor Tom	67	High Agogo
44	Pedal Hi-Hat	68	Low Agogo
45	Low Tom	69	Cabasa
46	Open Hi-Hat	70	Maracas
47	Low Mid Tom	71	Short Whistle
48	High Mid Tom	72	Long Whistle
49	Crash Cymbal	73	Short Guiro
50	High Tom	74	Long Guiro
51	Ride Cymbal 1	75	Claves
52	Chinese Cymbal	76	High Woodblock
53	Ride Bell	77	Low Woodblock
54	Tambourine	78	Mute Cuica
55	Splash Cymbal	79	Open Cuica
56	Cowbell	80	Mute Triangle
57	Crash Cymbal 2	81	Open Triangle
58	Vibraslap		

chapter 4

introducing sequencers

MIDI sequencing is the area in which MIDI really gets interesting. MIDI sequencing makes it possible for us to record and play multipart MIDI compositions in any style, from techno to classical. A modern MIDI sequencer might more accurately be called a multitrack MIDI recorder, but the term sequencer seems to have stuck. In the context of recording in general, the term 'track' refers to a means of recording a musical part in such a way that it may be edited, erased or re-recorded independently of the other parts. If you're familiar with the concept of multitrack tape, working with MIDI sequencing will appear quite familiar. Traditional musicians might prefer to visualise a sequencer track as being roughly equivalent to one part of music in a multipart score. A typical MIDI sequencer will provide a bare minimum of 16 tracks, and will often include many more. Why we should require more than 16 sequencer tracks when we have only 16 MIDI channels will be explained in due course.

musical layers

Using a MIDI sequencer, numerous separate musical parts can be recorded at different times, either by playing the parts one at a time on a MIDI keyboard, by entering note and timing data manually, or through a combination of live playing and editing. The individual parts may be monophonic or they may comprise chords, and it is up to the individual how much is recorded on each track. In fact, a difficult part could be split over two or more tracks set to the same MIDI channel and then recorded in several takes. For example, a piano player with limited skill might first record the left hand part on one track and then later record the right hand part on a different track. This is just one reason why you might need more than 16 sequencer tracks. Once recorded, these parts may be played back via any MIDI-compatible synthesiser or a collection of synthesisers.

Unless you have a sequencer with a built-in synthesiser, it can't play back any sounds on its own. Instead the sequencer is used to control one or more synthesisers, and the number of different musical parts that can be played back at once is limited by the number and type and synthesisers you have. Fortunately, most modern synths and PC soundcards are capable of playing back up to 16 different sounds at once, each controlled by a different MIDI channel, and so even a single synth will allow you to create quite ambitious sequences.

composing with MIDI

Having never written a symphony I can't detail the exact process, but I expect it goes something like this: the composer sits at the piano, testing musical ideas, and the ones that are deemed viable are then written down on manuscript paper for the various sections of the orchestra to play. The composer imagines the parts already written down while adding new sections, harmonies and so on, and when the score is nominally finished it will be scrutinised and any required alterations will be made. Once the score is complete, an orchestra will then be engaged to play the composition based on the score written by the composer. Essentially, the composer, who may or may not be able to perform to an acceptable standard on an instrument, has conceived a piece of music and then written a list of instructions in the form of a musical score so that a musically proficient orchestra can perform it.

So how does this relate to the way in which the MIDI composer writes? As with the orchestral composer the work usually starts at the keyboard, but this time the keyboard is a MIDI instrument connected to a sequencer, not a piano. Instead of writing down a score, the composer will record sections of the music into the sequencer against an electronic metronome set to the desired tempo, and instead of scanning a score to verify what's been done he or she will simply play back the recording via a suitable synthesiser to hear exactly what has been recorded. Those composers who can't play well enough to record the various parts in real time can enter notes directly into the sequencer in much the same way as a composer would write notes onto manuscript paper. It's tedious and time consuming, but it can be done.

benefits of MIDI

Perhaps the best reason for using a MIDI sequencer is that there is no need to hire an orchestra or a band of session musicians; even a relatively inexpensive multitimbral synthesiser will provide all of the sounds you will need. In some ways the sequencer is better than the written score, in that it can play back a part exactly as you played it in the first place, and it doesn't have to quantise everything to equal subdivisions of a musical bar as the written score does – though it can if you want it to. Also, as with a score, if you're not happy with something you've written you don't have to start from scratch: you can just erase the unwanted notes and 'write' in new ones.

When summarising the way in which a musician composes using a sequencer, it's clear that there isn't really much difference from the way in which a traditional composer works. Both composers are likely to edit their compositions to some degree before they're entirely happy with them, and both bring in performers to play the finished composition. It doesn't really matter whether the finished piece is played by a bank of synths or by a hired orchestra, whose role is simply to reproduce the composer's original work as faithfully as possible.

MIDI and sequencing

In much the same way that a musical score is a series of instructions to the musicians, the finished MIDI sequence contains a series of instructions which tell the synthesisers exactly what to play and when to play it. The MIDI sequence is, if you like, the electronic equivalent of the player piano, or pianola, mentioned earlier, in which a punched paper roll holds the instructions that determine exactly what the piano plays. The essential difference between the two is that, with MIDI, the punched paper roll is replaced by computer memory and computer disks capable of controlling the output of a number of different instruments at the same time.

sequencer setup

In a typical setup, a master MIDI controller (usually a keyboard, but not always) is connected to a sequencer via a MIDI cable, and when this sequencer is set to record then any notes played on the keyboard are recorded as MIDI data into whichever sequencer track has been selected for recording. In a simple system there might be 16 MIDI tracks set up so that each is on a different MIDI channel, and if the MIDI output of the sequencer is fed to a 16-part multitimbral module then all 16 tracks can be played back at once. If only an eight-part multitimbral module is available then only eight different sounds can be played back at once, in the same way that a real-life eight-piece ensemble can only play a maximum of eight different lines of music at the same time. Figure 4.1 shows a typical computer-based sequencing system.

If you have a keyboard that includes a synth, as in the diagram, simply select Local Off and connect it up like any other synth module. Local Off isolates the synth's keyboard from its sound-generating circuitry so that, in effect, it behaves as if it were a separate dumb keyboard and MIDI synth module. This is necessary to prevent MIDI information being fed around the system in a continuous loop, which usually causes trouble. (See the 'Troubleshooting' section at the end of this chapter.)

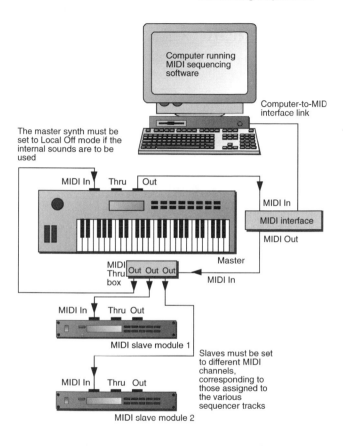

Figure 4.1: Basic sequencing setup

click track

Although you could treat a sequencer as no more than a multitrack recorder for MIDI information, its real power is evident in the way in which it can modify or edit recorded data. When a recording is made, the sequencer is normally set to the tempo of the desired recording and a metronome click is created in order that the musical performance can be synchronised with the internal tempo of the sequencer. Working in this way, the MIDI data is arranged in musically meaningful bars, which makes editing the timing of notes or copying and moving whole sections both easy and precise.

When writing music with changes in tempo, it is generally possible to enter a new tempo at any bar and beat location. More sophisticated sequencers may even have a graphic tempo-editing mode in which curves can be drawn to create smooth increases or decreases in tempo.

If you don't want to be tied to tempo at all, you can simply turn off the metronome click and play as you would when using a tape recorder. The practical disadvantage of working this way is that you can't use the internal beat and bar structure to plan your edits, and you can't use the quantise function as the timing of your performance will be quite independent of the sequencer's internal tempo clock.

quantising

One important feature common to both hardware and software sequencers is their ability to quantise data after it is recorded, and this is a useful feature for those users not possessed of a perfect sense of timing. Essentially, when you choose to quantise something, the timing is changed in order to push each note you've recorded to the nearest exact subdivision of a bar. For example, if you are working in 4/4 time and you select 16 as your quantise value, every note moves to the nearest point on an invisible grid dividing the bar into 16 equal time slots.

Quantise must be used carefully as it can strip all of the 'feel' from some types of music. However, if you're working on a piece of dance music, in which precise timing is essential, the quantise function is indispensable. It's worth bearing in mind that quantising will only produce meaningful results if your original recording was made in time with the metronome click of the sequencer. Furthermore, if your timing is really out you may find that, when you quantise, the occasional note snaps to a position one step away from that to which you originally intended it to go. Quantising always pushes notes to the nearest quantise step, and if your badly-timed note was more than half a step out it will be quantised to the wrong step!

The more recent computer packages allow you to unquantise data as well as quantise it, but some less advanced software sequencers and a number of hardware sequencers perform what is known as destructive quantise, so it's important to keep a copy of the original if you think you'll need to make any changes to the track.

On more sophisticated sequencers you'll find a percentage quantise option that allows the notes you've played to be shifted towards the exact quantise division by a percentage. For example, if you set the quantise value at 50% the note will move to a position halfway between the position at which you actually played it and the position of the nearest quantise division. This is a great way of tightening up your playing without making it sound too mechanical.

Another quantise-related function is swing. With swing, the quantise grid is moved away from regularly-spaced slots to alternating longer and shorter slots. This can be used subtly to add 'feel', or used more aggressively to turn a 4/4 track into a 2/4 track.

tracks and channels

At this point in the proceedings it's very easy to get MIDI channels and sequencer tracks mixed up, but they are not the same thing. A sequencer track is simply somewhere to record one layer of your composition, but the MIDI information on that track can be on any MIDI channel you want it to be. A track can even contain MIDI information relating to two or more MIDI channels, although, to prevent confusion, most of the time a single track records data on a single channel.

It's also possible to have several different tracks recording MIDI data set to the same channel. For example, if you're recording a complicated drum part you might want to put the bass and snare drum on one track, the cymbals and hi-hats on another and any tom fills on a third. All of the drum sounds may be on the same MIDI channel, but because they're on different tracks they're effectively recorded as different layers. Not only does this make the parts easier to play but it also makes them less confusing to edit if you want to make any changes. Figure 4.2 shows the arrange page of a popular computer-based sequencing package, showing the layout of the tracks and the way in which recorded sequences are represented.

rechannelling

On early sequencers, every time you wanted to record a part on a different MIDI channel you had to select a

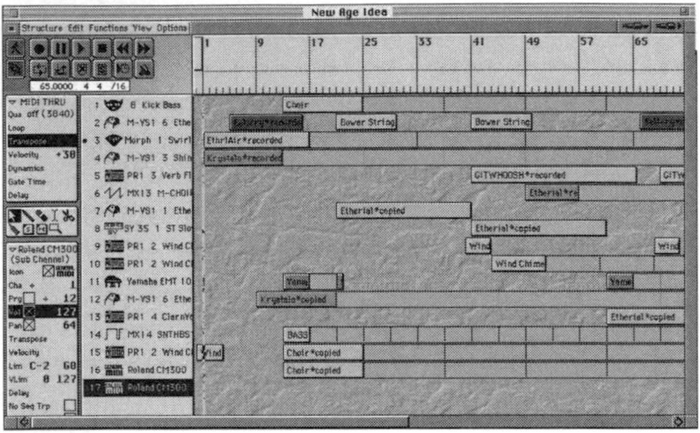

Figure 4.2: Sequencer arrange pages

new MIDI channel on the master keyboard. This proved tedious when you had to constantly hop from one part in the music to another, so to get around this modern sequencers convert the incoming MIDI data to the appropriate channel for the track on which you're recording. This is known as rechannelling. To use a postal analogy, the sequencer intercepts the MIDI messages as they come in, re-addresses them by changing their MIDI channel and then sends them on to their new destinations. This is another feat that's accomplished without any intervention from the user, and it makes life very easy because, once you've completed recording one track, all you need do is select the next one and play.

cut, copy and paste

In some respects, a MIDI sequencer bears more resemblance to a word processor than anything else. Like a word processor, you can delete or replace wrong characters (in this case musical notes), and if you want to use the same phrase more than once you can copy it and paste copies into new locations so that you don't have to repeat the same phrase a number of times. For example, if a song has the same structure for each chorus you need only play the chorus once and then copy it to any bar location where you'd like it to be repeated. What's more, you don't have to copy all of the tracks – you could simply copy sections of the drum track, or perhaps the keyboard pad part. Usually this is done graphically, on-screen, by grabbing sections of the track with the mouse and dragging them to new locations. Long sections can be broken up into smaller sections using on-screen tools, often represented by a icon resembling a pair of scissors.

We've already seen that MIDI information comprises not just note information but also controller data from modulation wheels, pitch-bend wheels, expression pedals and so forth. Unless you deliberately filter out certain types of MIDI data (and some sequencers have the facility to do this), you'll find that your sequencer captures Note On, Note Off, velocity, pitch, modulation, aftertouch and other controller information as well as MIDI Program Change and Bank Change messages. A useful trick when recording a part that needs a lot of complicated pitch bending or vibrato is to record the part straight onto one track and then record the vibrato and pitch-bend data on another set to the same MIDI channel. As you record the controller data track, you'll hear it also affecting the performance on the original track.

A sequencer track must also be told which synthesiser sound it is expected to control, and so, in addition to the MIDI channel (which tells it which instrument or which part of a multitimbral instrument it is controlling), it is also necessary to enter the program number of the patch you want to hear and, if the synthesiser supports MIDI Bank Change messages, you also need to tell it in which bank the sound is located. For this reason it helps to photocopy the relevant patch lists from your synth manuals and pin them to the wall close to your sequencer.

A MIDI program change recorded during the count-in period of a track will ensure that the synth being used for that track switches to the correct patch before playing commences. However, you can also insert program changes partway through a track if you want to change the sound for a solo, for example. This is the MIDI equivalent of writing a note on the score at a certain bar number to tell a violin player to put down his violin and play the next part on a flute. Although this isn't something you'd usually do in real life, a MIDI module is equally proficient on all instruments and, as yet, MIDI modules don't have trades unions!

playback

When the MIDI sequence is played back the sequencer transmits the MIDI information to the receiving synthesiser in exactly the same order and with the same timing as it was originally played, though it is possible to change the tempo after recording without affecting the pitch (unlike a tape recorder, in which case you're dealing with sound rather than MIDI data). If you're still not sure why the pitch doesn't increase as the tempo increases, think back to the orchestra and score analogy: if the conductor asks for a piece to be played faster, the orchestral instruments don't change in pitch. Similarly, if you pedal a pianola faster, the paper roll will be moving faster but the piano's tuning will remain the same.

In reality MIDI has a finite timing resolution because the computer has to work to an internal timing routine based on an electronic clock, but in practice MIDI is far more accurate than a human performer and is capable of resolving a bar of music into at least 960 time divisions, and frequently more.

sequence editing

In the editing pages of a typical sequencer it is possible to change the value, start time, length and velocity of any of the notes you've played, or you can build up compositions by entering the notes manually and placing new notes onto the quantise grid in non-real time, rather like writing out manuscript. If you have a package with a scoring facility, it's also possible to enter notes directly onto the score.

destructive and non-destructive

Although quantising is irreversible on some budget sequencers and sequencing packages, all professional systems will allow you to unquantise something at a later time if required. In fact, many reversing procedures are made possible because the originally-recorded data isn't actually changed at all – you only hear changes because the data is processed in real time as the sequence is played back. Such features are said to be non-destructive because the original performance data is left intact. Though this makes the computer running your sequencer work harder it also means that you are free to experiment with less risk of doing anything irreversible. Of course you should save your work regularly, so if something does go wrong you can go back to the previous save and pick up the work from there.

A number of other related non-destructive editing options are often available, including the ability to transpose your music (either as you play or after recording), the ability to make the music louder or softer by adjusting the overall velocity, and the ability to use the same piece of data at different points within the same song. On some systems you can even compress the dynamic range of your MIDI data to even out the difference between the louder notes and the softer ones.

It may also be possible to delay or advance tracks relative to each other in order to change the feel of a piece of music. For example, using a negative delay to pull a snare drum beat forward will help make the track drive along, whereas delaying the snare will make the beat lay back.

Of course, some edits are destructive as the changes may be permanent. For example, moving a note to a new time or pitch is a destructive edit, as is erasing or adding a note. Even so, there's usually an 'undo' function that allows you to reverse the last procedure you performed, destructive or not.

MIDI drums

It's possible to sequence your drum machine, just as you can with any other type of MIDI sound module, but first you'll have to turn off the drum machine's external MIDI synchronisation or every time you turn on your sequencer the drum machine's internal patterns will start to play. Unlike a conventional MIDI instrument, on which each note plays a different pitch of the same sound, drum machines place different sounds on different keys, thereby allowing access to many different drum sounds.

Because it's difficult to play a complete drum part in one go on a keyboard, it's common practise to spread the drums over several sequencer tracks so that, for example, the bass and snare can be recorded first, the hi-hats next and then the fills. This makes it easy to edit drum tracks without having to work out which note relates to which drum sound, but once the drum part is completed the tracks can be conveniently merged into one.

types of sequencer

All MIDI sequencers are based on computer technology, but you can choose between buying a sequencer system that runs on an existing computer (such as an Atari ST, Apple Mac, Apple PowerMac, IBM PC or Commodore Amiga) or opting for a piece of dedicated hardware in which everything you need is built into one box. The two varieties work in a similar manner; what tends to vary is the way in which the recorded information is displayed and how easily it can be edited. Hardware sequencers also come built into workstation-type keyboard synthesisers, and some hardware sequencers have built-in synthesiser modules.

For those who are relatively accomplished players hardware sequencers offer the benefits of simplicity and convenience, but because they don't have the ability to display as much information display as a full-sized computer screen, and because there's no mouse editing is generally less comprehensive and more time consuming than it would be on a computer-based system. However, the recording and playback of tracks is usually very straightforward. Hardware sequencers are often more practical for live performing – they are more compact and more rugged than a computer, as there is no cumbersome monitor and fewer things to plug in.

MIDI data storage

It's one thing recording a MIDI sequence, but what do you do with it once it's finished? There's no manuscript paper to store your work on – instead your song data is stored as a MIDI song file on a floppy disk or hard drive. Some MIDI sequencers (including all of the computer-based varieties) lose their stored information when they are switched off, so it is vital that you save your work to disk at regular intervals. Computers occasionally crash, always when you're least expecting it, so don't wait until you've finished a day's work before saving it. Save your work every few minutes.

A single floppy disk will hold several songs of average complexity, and most hardware sequencers have a built-in disk drive for this purpose. However, some low-cost models use memory with a battery backup instead of disks, and once the memory is full you have to either save your work to a MIDI data filer (which has an built-in drive) or erase your old project before you can start a new one. Usually this kind of sequencer can store only a few songs at a time, so a model with a built-in drive is preferable.

computer complexity

The computer-based sequencer is capable of more sophistication than most hardware models, which means that there may be a steeper learning curve. You must also familiarise yourself with the general operation of the computer before trying to tackle a sequencer package. However, in my opinion this is compensated by the amount of visual feedback available, which makes things especially easy when it comes to creating new song arrangements or editing previously-recorded material.

MIDI interface

With a hardware sequencer you simply plug your master keyboard into the MIDI In socket, plug a synthesiser into the MIDI Out socket and you're ready to go. Computers, on the other hand, don't usually have MIDI sockets, the obvious exception being the still popular (but now ageing) Atari ST. This means that, unless you're using an Atari, you'll need to buy an external MIDI interface and a PC soundcard with a built-in MIDI interface, or you could use one of the synth modules that comes with a built-in MIDI interface. To use a computer for MIDI, you'll therefore need a MIDI interface as well as suitable sequencing software.

MIDI interfaces for older Apple Macintosh machines plug into the modem or printer ports at the back of the computer, while the G3 models and above use the USB (Universal Serial Buss) interface. PC users need either an interface card that is fitted inside the computer or an external plug-in interface. Most PC soundcards include a MIDI interface facility, though it may be necessary to buy a special adaptor cable to make use of it.

user interface

The majority of the leading software sequencing packages have adopted the style of interface pioneered by Steinberg in their Cubase software. The success of this interface is that it uses a multitrack tape analogy, where the sequencer tracks are depicted as individual strips arranged vertically, with musical bars running from left to right. Once a section of a track has been recorded it shows up as a building brick, running from the record start bar location to the record end bar location. This sequence may then be dragged, using the computer's mouse, to a new position in the same track, or it may even be moved to a completely different track so that it plays back with a different sound. Sequence blocks may also be copied, split into shorter sections or deleted as required.

Most software sequencers comprise a main page, for handling basic recording and arranging, along with a number of further pages which address various aspects of editing and scoring (where applicable). The record and playback controls are invariably designed to look something like a tape recorder's transport control buttons, and the edit pages usually allow you to examine and change the recorded data as a list of MIDI events, either graphically as a 'piano roll' grid display or as a conventional musical score. Most sequencers also have the facility to graphically edit controller information. Figure 4.3 shows some of the edit pages from a popular software sequencer.

Some computer software sequencing packages also include sophisticated score-writing facilities which enable you to print out your compositions in the form of sheet music, in which case you'll need a printer which is compatible both with your computer and the software package. However, some musical literacy is useful because the computer doesn't always interpret what you play in the same way that a trained score writer would.

overview

MIDI sequencers are very powerful tools for both composing and recording music, and because they have become so sophisticated there are still many things that I haven't discussed. For example, MIDI allows you to remotely control the volume of your synths, and so by

```
                    New Age Id...:Etherial*copied
 ■ Edit Functions View
        POSITION          STATUS   CHA   NUM  VAL   LENGTH/INFO
 ------------- Start of List -------------
        21   1   1   1    NOTE      1    B1   25    3   3   1 220
        21   1   1   1    NOTE      1    E2   32    3   3   1 216
        21   1   1   1    NOTE      1   G#2   12    3   3   1  80
        21   1   1   1    NOTE      1   C#3   17    3   3   1 168
        21   1   1   1    NOTE      1   D#3   18    3   3   1  60
        25   1   1   1    NOTE      1   G#1  103    3   3   3 232
        25   1   1   1    NOTE      1    E2  103    3   3   3 232
        25   1   1   1    NOTE      1   G#2  103    3   3   3 232
        25   1   1   1    NOTE      1   D#3  103    3   3   3 232
        25   1   1   1    NOTE      1   G#3  103    3   3   3 232
        29   1   1   1    NOTE      1   F#1   97    3   3   3  52
        29   1   1   1    NOTE      1   D#2   97    3   3   3  52
        29   1   1   1    NOTE      1   C#3   97    3   3   3  52
        33   1   1   1    NOTE      1   G#1   97    3   3   3  52
        33   1   1   1    NOTE      1   C#2   97    3   3   3  52
        33   1   1   1    NOTE      1   A#2   97    3   3   3  52
        37   1   1   1    NOTE      1    B1   97    3   3   3  52
        37   1   1   1    NOTE      1    E2   97    3   3   3  52
        37   1   1   1    NOTE      1   G#2   97    3   3   3  52
        37   1   1   1    NOTE      1   C#3   97    3   3   3  52
        37   1   1   1    NOTE      1    B3   97    3   3   3  52
 -------------- End of List --------------
```

Figure 4.3: Sequencer edit pages

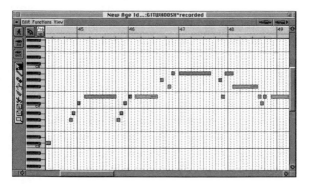

Figure 4.3: Sequencer edit pages

recording MIDI volume information you can create automated mixes. Similarly, you can also automate the pan positions of the various parts in a mix.

Wonderful as sequencers are, however, they are still far from perfect devices. Aside from the inevitable software bugs that creep in, they force you to work in a way that you probably wouldn't if you were playing and composing conventionally. Most insidious is the metronome, or tempo click, with which you have to play along, and although you can turn this off and record 'free' regardless of bar positions you then won't be able to quantise your data and you won't be able to print out a meaningful score. This means that tempo changes have to be planned rather than inserted spontaneously, and although software designers are now including features to help in this area (such as rebarring) it takes a lot of determination to move away from the fixed-tempo, four-to-the-bar music to which we've all become so accustomed.

Despite these pitfalls, MIDI sequencing still offers many more advantages than disadvantages, and used creatively it allows many possibilities that would have been far too impractical or expensive in the pre-MIDI era. Once you've started using it and seen how easy it is to handle the basics, you'll wonder why those software manuals have to be so thick!

hardware versus software

Software sequencers have several obvious advantages over hardware sequencers, but that doesn't mean that they're better – it all depends on the facilities you need and whether or not you want your sequencer to be portable. Software sequencers have a good visual interface and more comprehensive editing facilities, on top of which you can still use the computer for other purposes. Furthermore, you're not tied to one software manufacturer – you can pick whatever suits you the best.

It is also true that most computer sequencers support multiple MIDI output ports via a special multiport MIDI interface (see the section on 'MIDI Ports' below). This means that the user is no longer restricted to 16 MIDI channels – a typical system will provide six or more output ports, providing over 96 MIDI channels to work with. In contrast, the majority of hardware sequencers support only one or two MIDI output ports.

MIDI ports

A basic MIDI interface provides a single MIDI output socket, so that a maximum of 16 MIDI channels will be available. However, you may want to use two or more multitimbral synthesisers to create a composition with more than 16 parts, or (as is more often the case) if you have several synthesiser modules you may want to change from one to the other without having to reconnect MIDI leads. This can be achieved by using a MIDI interface with multiple output ports, which in effect constitutes physically-separate MIDI Outs that can each source 16 MIDI channels of data.

You can never have more than 16 MIDI channels, but if you use a multiport MIDI interface in conjunction with compatible sequencing software you will, in effect, have several different sets of 16 MIDI channels. The ports may be designated by number or letter within the sequencer so that there are 16 channels on port A, another 16 on port B, a further 16 on port C and so on. By connecting a different 16-part multitimbral synth module to each port of a four-port interface you can have 64 different sound sources, each of which can be addressed individually be specifying a MIDI channel along with a port number (A, B, C or D). Figure 4.4 illustrates how such a multiport system might be configured. It is important to realise that the multiport interface and the sequencing software must be compatible. A list of suitable interfaces should be listed in the sequencer manual, but if you are in any doubt at all you should consult your dealer.

Hardware-based sequencers usually have only one or two output ports, and this lack of scope for expansion is one of their greatest limitations in a complex MIDI setup. Future designers of sequencers will hopefully realise this problem and design in facilities for port expansion in later models, or at the very least support for external MIDI multiport interfaces.

file format

Though MIDI sequence data is stored in a file format specific to the software manufacturer, some of the more popular sequencing packages allow you to transfer song data from one computer platform to

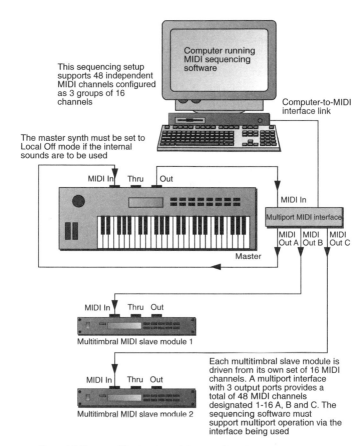

This sequencing setup supports 48 independent MIDI channels configured as 3 groups of 16 channels

Computer running MIDI sequencing software

Computer-to-MIDI interface link

The master synth must be set to Local Off mode if the internal sounds are to be used

MIDI In   Thru   Out

MIDI In

Multiport MIDI interface

MIDI Out A   MIDI Out B   MIDI Out C

Master

MIDI In   Thru   Out

Multitimbral MIDI slave module 1

Each multitimbral slave module is driven from its own set of 16 MIDI channels. A multiport interface with 3 output ports provides a total of 48 MIDI channels designated 1-16 A, B and C. The sequencing software must support multiport operation via the interface being used

MIDI In   Thru   Out

Multitimbral MIDI slave module 2

Figure 4.4: How a multiport system might be configured

another and, in some cases, even from one manufacturer's software sequencer to another's. Even in those cases that they don't, it's still possible to save your work as a Standard MIDI file and transfer it that way, although this only works for a maximum of 16 tracks at a time. Computer-based systems also allow you to print out the score of your compositions.

Hardware-based sequencers are generally more reliable than computers in live situations and are considerably more portable. They also offer a one-box solution, are physically quieter than a typical computer (with no noisy fans or whirring drives), and there's also no monitor screen to cause interference when you want to play your electric guitar in the studio.

main sequencer features

What basic features can you expect from a MIDI sequencer? Every sequencer is obviously different, but all should be capable of the following core functions:

- Real-time recording, via which a MIDI performance can be played in real-time from a keyboard and recorded in much the same way as on a tape recorder. Unlike a tape recorder, however, you can transpose, change tempo, pick a different synth sound and quantise your data after recording. If you want to use the quantise feature you will have to play against the internal metronome track.

- Step-time recording, via which notes are played in one note at a time – rather like typing a letter with one finger! You decide where the notes go and how long they're going to be, after which you can play back your work at any tempo. In practice, most people use mainly real-time recording with occasional recourse to step time when the going gets tough. With a piano-roll-type editing screen, it is also possible to draw your notes directly onto the quantise grid and then use the mouse pointer to stretch them to their required lengths. A package with scoring facilities will allow you to place conventional musical symbols onto a stave.

- Synchronisation facilities. Though it is possible to compose music entirely by sequencer, it's sometimes useful to be able to use a drum machine, tape recorder or hard-disk recorder at the same time. In order to synchronise the tempo of a sequencer to that of another MIDI device or tape machine equipped with a suitable sync interface the sequencer must be equipped with sync facilities, and these are sometimes omitted on very cheap sequencing software. There are several synchronising options, but the most commonly used are MIDI clock, as already discussed, and MTC (MIDI Time Code).

* Multiport interface support. In a complex MIDI system, one set of 16 MIDI channels may not be enough. A multiport MIDI interface compatible with the sequencing software will provide up to eight separate MIDI outputs, each with its own set of 16 MIDI channels. Note, however, that this should not be confused with a simple multi-output interface, through which multiple output sockets carry duplicates of the same MIDI data. These are really just a combination of a single-port interface and a MIDI Thru box.

* File import. MIDI sequencers usually save song data in a proprietary format which other sequencers may not be able to read. Some of the more advanced software systems boast the ability to load and import song files from other sequencers, but a more common method of file transfer is to use the SMF (Standard MIDI File) format. SMFs were devised to allow complete interchangeability between MIDI song files, and they also make it possible for third-party companies to provide commercial sequencer files that can be read by any

machine. However, SMFs can only handle the basic 16 MIDI channels and not multiport data.

Be aware, however, that, although the file format may be standard, the floppy disk formats used by different computers aren't always interchangeable. For example, Atari STs and PCs can read disks of the same format (though the ST can't handle high-density disks) but Apple Macs can only read PC disks if they are running either System 7.5 software or upwards or if they are equipped with a PC-to-Mac file-exchange program, such as AccessPC. Hardware sequencers may have their own disk formats, in which case MIDI song files can only be loaded if they are stored on disks that have been formatted on the same type of machine.

Along with the facilities mentioned above, a typical sequencer will also be equipped with a number of editing tools to enable you to modify your composition after recording. These range from the ability to change individual notes to the ability to change entire arrangements and swap instruments. The main editing operations are listed below.

•   Quantising. This is the ability to move your notes to the nearest accurate subdivision of a bar (for example, 16ths of a bar). The user can set the number of subdivisions in a bar prior to quantising.

* Transposition. Notes can be transposed by any amount without altering their lengths, and entire compositions or sections of compositions can easily be shifted to a different key.

* Copy, cut and paste. Any section of music can be copied to different tracks or to different locations in the song. This is a useful function for duplicating repeated sections such as choruses, or for doubling up a line of music on two tracks by copying a part and then assigning the copy to a different instrument. The cut function allows the removal of any unwanted material.

* Mute. Most sequencers allow you to mute a number of tracks at once, which means that you can record several tracks and then mute some, making it possible to listen to only the ones you want. This is useful if you've just played three solos but you're not sure which was the best.

* Solo. This function mutes all of the other tracks you have recorded so that you can hear the soloed track in isolation.

- Cycle. This simply allows you to continually loop a specific section of music while you record or edit, which can be useful for rehearsing parts prior to recording

- Undo. If provided, the undo function will allow you to reverse the last operation. Usually there is only one level of undo, although a few systems provide multiple levels.

MIDI problems

The starting point of a basic MIDI sequencing setup is the keyboard. It's here that the MIDI information originates. The master keyboard is connected via its MIDI Out to the MIDI In of the MIDI interface or directly to the MIDI In of the hardware sequencer or computer. As mentioned earlier, if the keyboard includes a synth section (in other words, if it makes sounds) then switch to Local Off and patch a MIDI cable from the sequencer's MIDI Out to the keyboard's MIDI In. If there are other MIDI modules in the system then you can daisy-chain them in any order by feeding the MIDI Thru of one piece of equipment directly to the MIDI In of another or by using a Thru box. If the master keyboard doesn't have a Local Off facility, consult your sequencer manual to see if you can disable the MIDI Thru on the channel to which your master keyboard is set (most sequencers provide for this eventuality).

Up to three modules can normally be daisy-chained in this Thru-to-In setup without problems, but if the chain is any longer you may suffer stuck or missed notes due to corruption of the MIDI signal. In this case you should attach a multiple-output MIDI Thru box to the output of your sequencer and then feed each module, or short chains of two or three modules, from separate outputs on the Thru box.

MIDI timing

MIDI has a finite timing resolution because the computer's internal timing routine is based on an electronic clock. However, MIDI is still far more accurate than a human performer at keeping time, and is capable of resolving a 4/4 bar of music into at least 960 time divisions. Some software extends this to an even finer degree, but this can cause timing problems in some situations.

If too much MIDI data is sent at once you may get a musical traffic jam, causing the notes to be spread out slightly. This may be particularly noticeable if you have a large number of notes quantised to the same beat (for example, all 16 channels set to play a large chord at exactly the same time). Using other MIDI controller data can also slow things up, but the better sequencing software packages help to reduce this problem by assigning priority to note timing.

If you encounter problems with MIDI timing, there are steps you can take. Because the first track is usually the first to be dealt with in terms of timing, one trick is to put the most time-sensitive parts, such as drums, onto the first few tracks and less critical instruments, such as slow-attack strings, onto the later tracks. Timing problems may also occur with older keyboards and instruments which are slow to send out or respond to information. Some of the early MIDI keyboards took around 10ms to send a MIDI message after a key had been depressed, and some of the slower modules took that long to respond to an incoming MIDI Note message. Modern instruments generally have a faster response time, but some models are still noticeably faster than others.

Another trick is to apply a little negative track delay to those tracks carrying slow attack sounds, such as strings or brass, so that the notes fire fractionally earlier than the rest of the quantised material.

checklist

If you've connected up your system as described but no
sound comes out, here are a few things to check:

- Verify that everything is switched on and that your
  synth modules are set to Multi or Sequencer mode
  (assuming you want to use them multitimbrally).
  Also, make sure your synths are set to the same MIDI
  channels to those on which you're sending data.

- Check your MIDI cable connections and don't rule
  out the possibility of a faulty MIDI lead. Some
  modules have a combined MIDI Out/Thru socket,
  and if this is the case ensure that MIDI Thru is
  enabled (consult the handbook relating to that
  particular piece of equipment). To help narrow down
  the source of the problem, most sequencers have
  some form of indication that they're receiving MIDI
  data, and many modules have an LED or some other
  indicator which blinks when data is being received.

- Check that Omni mode is switched off on all
  modules (Poly mode is that most commonly used).
  If you notice two or more instruments trying to play
  the same part, the chances are that you've either set
  more than one module to the same MIDI channel
  or that something's been left set to Omni mode. If

your master keyboard plays its own sounds whenever you try to record on any track or channel, check that Local Off is really selected, as on some instruments Local Off reverts to Local On every time the power is switched on.

• If you play a single note and are treated to a burst of sound rather like machine-gun fire, or if you have problems with stuck notes or apparently limited polyphony, the chances are that you have a MIDI loop. In a MIDI loop, MIDI data generated by the master keyboard passes through the sequencer and is somehow shunted back to the input of the master keyboard, where it starts its round trip all over again, in much the same manner of acoustic feedback. This usually happens when a keyboard synth is used as a master keyboard and Local Off has not been selected.

If you have one of those rare instruments with no Local Off facility, try disabling the sequencer MIDI Thru on the channel on which your master keyboard is sending data (which most people leave set to channel one).

If you are unfortunate enough to have neither facility, all you can do is record with the MIDI In disconnected from your master keyboard and use the sounds from external modules. If you wish, once you have finished recording you can reconnect the master keyboard's MIDI In and use it to play back one of the recorded parts or to layer it with an existing synth voice.

chapter 5

MIDI synchronisation

Most modern software sequencers allow you to use a computer hard drive as a multitrack recorder, which can be accessed from within your sequencer software. This is a very attractive way to work for the musician who wishes to add the occasional vocal and guitar overdubs to a primarily MIDI recording, and with backup facilities such as recordable DVD now available it is also attractive for those working on larger-scale projects.

However, there may still be occasions when you want to use use multitrack tape or a stand-alone tapeless recorder alongside your sequencer, and although you could simply record your sequenced MIDI instruments onto the multitrack machine before adding your vocals, guitars and so on, this isn't necessarily the most effective way to work. Multitrack recorders are limited in the number of tracks they provide, and it is often necessary to keep all MIDI material separate until the final mix.

The ideal solution is to find a way of having the MIDI sequencer and tape machine running in perfect sync with each other. The sequenced sounds can then be fed into the final mix without having been recorded on multitrack in the first place. In this way it is possible to change the sounds on MIDI instruments right up until the moment before mixing.

In the film industry, cine film and magnetic audio tape was originally kept in sync by means of sprocket holes cut into the edges of the film and tape. These passed over toothed cogs fitted to the same shaft so that, once the film and tape were lined up, they were always synchronised. MIDI provides us with a simple means of achieving the same results electronically.

time codes

One method is to record a MIDI synchronisation code onto one track of the multitrack recorder. This code is composed of a series of pulses that perform the same function as the sprocket holes in cine film. Using this method means that one track is used up in recording the necessary sync code, but it also means that you gain as many 'virtual' tracks as your sequencer and synth/sound module collection can provide. For example, if a MIDI sequencer were synchronised to

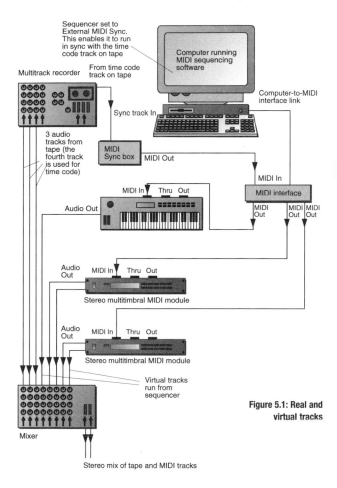

Sequencer set to
External MIDI Sync.
This enables it to run
in sync with the time
code track on tape

Computer running
MIDI sequencing
software

Multitrack recorder

From time code
track on tape

Computer-to-MIDI
interface link

Sync track In

3 audio
tracks from
tape (the
fourth track
is used for
time code)

MIDI
Sync box

MIDI Out

MIDI In

MIDI In   Thru   Out

MIDI interface

MIDI
Out

MIDI
Out

MIDI
Out

Audio Out

Audio
Out

MIDI In   Thru   Out

Stereo multitimbral MIDI module

Audio
Out

MIDI In   Thru   Out

Stereo multitimbral MIDI module

Virtual tracks
run from
sequencer

Mixer

Stereo mix of tape and MIDI tracks

Figure 5.1: Real and
virtual tracks

119

run along with a four-track recorder, the sync code would take up one track, leaving you with three tracks for your audio. Figure 5.1 illustrates how this method works in practise. The concept is simple, but to understand it fully it's first necessary to know a little more about MIDI clock.

MIDI clock

MIDI sequencers and drum machines have an internal tempo clock, an invisible timing grid on which all notes or beats are superimposed. Think of MIDI clock as a high-resolution metronome: it provides the electronic sprockets and gears that allow two or more pieces of MIDI equipment to be run in perfect synchronisation, with one device acting as a master (and thus dictating the tempo) and the others functioning as slaves. For example, by using just MIDI clock it is possible to connect two drum machines so that both run in sync, to slave a sequencer to a drum machine, or to slave a drum machine to a sequencer. Also, with the aid of a suitable sync box, sequencers may also be synchronised to tape machines.

In physical terms, MIDI clock is a part of the data stream coming out the of the master device's MIDI Out socket, and so only a regular MIDI lead is required – no additional cables or connections. The MIDI Out of the master is linked to the MIDI In of the slave, and the master machine constantly sends out the MIDI clock signal at the tempo selected, regardless of whether it is started or stopped, so that any slave devices plugged into it will know at exactly which tempo to start running when a MIDI Start command is received.

MIDI Start, Stop and Continue messages are a part of the standard MIDI real-time messages protocol, and are automatically sent by the master device. Stopping the master prompts it to send a MIDI Stop command, which commands any slaves to also stop. The Continue command compels the machines to continue playing from the point at which they were stopped. A MIDI Start message, on the other hand, always causes the song to start from the beginning.

external sync

To set up sync between two MIDI devices, the master unit must be set to internal clock mode and the slave machine to external clock mode. Whenever the master machine starts, the slave will start automatically and will run in perfect sync with it. This is all very well if you simply want to run a drum machine and a sequencer together, but how does it work with a tape recorder?

In this case, what's needed is a device that fools a sequencer set to external sync (slave mode) into thinking that it's actually hooked up to a MIDI master device when it's actually connected to a tape machine. Not surprisingly, such a device is called a MIDI-to-tape sync unit, although it can also be used with tapeless recorders.

tape sync

Multitrack audio recorders can't record MIDI signals directly, so MIDI-to-tape sync has to convert MIDI clock timing data into a form that can be recorded. In practise there are several systems to choose from, although all convert the MIDI pulses into bursts of high-pitched sound. The system works by switching between two different frequencies, and, although this is quite clear to the user and requires no knowledge to operate, it's interesting to note that this system is known as FSK (Frequency Shift Keying).

A MIDI FSK sync box works something like this. After the sequence is written, a MIDI-to-tape sync unit is connected between the sequencer and multitrack machine. The sequence is then played back while the time code is recorded on one track of the recorder. The tempo of the song determines the speed of the MIDI clock and hence the tempo embedded in the time code.

To play back, you'd run the recorder, play the time code track back through the MIDI-to-tape sync unit, and patch its MIDI Out to the sequencer's MIDI In with the sequencer set to external MIDI sync mode. As soon as you run the tape from the start of the song the sequencer will start in sync with it. This system works fine – but only if you start at the beginning of the song every time. Figure 5.2 shows how a MIDI-to-tape sync unit is connected. This is clearly unsatisfactory if you want to work on a section a long way from the start. However, the Smart FSK system, as explained a little later in this chapter, gets around that problem.

time code and
tape noise reduction

Some types of noise reduction applied to analogue tapes can affect the reliability of time codes, so it is best to switch off the noise reduction on the sync track if at all possible. If the multitrack has a dedicated sync input and output, these will have been arranged to bypass the noise reduction and any EQ controls in order to allow a reliable recording to be made. You may need to experiment with the code level – if it is recorded too high it could bleed over to the adjacent tracks, making it audible in the final mix. Conversely, if it is recorded at too low a level it might not read reliably, causing the sequencer to hiccup or stop.

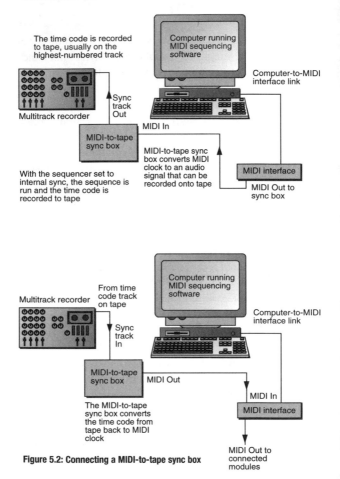

The time code is recorded to tape, usually on the highest-numbered track

Computer running MIDI sequencing software

Computer-to-MIDI interface link

Multitrack recorder

Sync track Out

MIDI-to-tape sync box

MIDI In

MIDI-to-tape sync box converts MIDI clock to an audio signal that can be recorded onto tape

MIDI interface

MIDI Out to sync box

With the sequencer set to internal sync, the sequence is run and the time code is recorded to tape

From time code track on tape

Multitrack recorder

Computer running MIDI sequencing software

Computer-to-MIDI interface link

Sync track In

MIDI-to-tape sync box

MIDI Out

MIDI In

MIDI interface

The MIDI-to-tape sync box converts the time code from tape back to MIDI clock

MIDI Out to connected modules

Figure 5.2: Connecting a MIDI-to-tape sync box

As a very general rule, dbx noise-reduction systems have the greatest effect on time code, whereas Dolby C doesn't seem to affect it at all. Unfortunately, some of the very early multitrackers only allow the noise reduction to be switched on or off globally for all four channels, which means that, if you want to work with a sync code, you'll have to put up with more tape hiss.

multitrack sync facilities

In order to use a sync unit with a multitrack analogue tape machine, it is vital that the machine either has a dedicated sync in and out or that it is possible to access the output from the sync track directly without needing to add it into the stereo mix, as you might have to with a budget cassette multitracker – time code is very unmusical! It is sometimes possible to work around the problem of not having a separate output for the sync track, but this usually involves a compromise of some kind or another. For example, with a tape machine that has only a single stereo output you could pan the three audio tracks to the left and the sync code to the right. The left output would then contain all of the audio information in mono while the right output would contain only the sync code. Depending on the machine, of course, it may also be possible to route the sync track to the outside world by using a pre-fade (sometimes called foldback) aux send and setting the channel fader level to zero. Of course, this also means that that particular aux send cannot be used for any other purpose.

smart FSK

Smart FSK is a distinct improvement over simple FSK systems. It works by using a piece of hidden MIDI information known as the MIDI SPP (Song Position Pointer). SPPs are invisible to the user, but most modern MIDI equipment recognises them so it is possible to forget all about them and let the computer or drum machine worry about them. In effect, SPPs tell MIDI devices where exactly in a song they're supposed to be. The advantage of using SPPs is that you can start the tape anywhere in the song and your slave sequencer will sync up at exactly the right place.

The practical advantage of all sync systems which use MIDI clock is that the tempo of the music is directly related to the clock rate of the sync code, which is created from the tempo of the original sequence. This means that any tempo changes in the original sequence will be followed automatically when the tape is run, and if the tape speeds up then so does the code, which in turn speeds up the sequencer. Unless anything more sophisticated is required, Smart FSK is the cheapest and most worry-free way of achieving sequencer-to-tape sync. It is also possible to use Smart FSK to sync a drum machine to tape if there is no sequencer available.

Smart FSK MIDI-to-tape sync units are relatively inexpensive, and they're manufactured by a number of companies. However, it's worth paying the extra on a unit with built-in MIDI merge because, without this facility, the MIDI In of your sequencer is occupied solely with reading time code, and therefore you can't record any new MIDI sequencer parts while the sequencer and tape machine are sync'ed up. However, if your sync box has a MIDI merge input you can plug your master keyboard into it and record new MIDI parts while the tape and sequencer are running in sync. This could be important when playing a part when you need to be able to hear the vocals or a taped guitar solo in order to get the right feel.

SMPTE

SMPTE is a synchronisation system which was originally developed for the film industry but is now also used in many musical applications. If you need to synchronise a sequencer to a videotape or film then some knowledge of SMPTE time code is essential. Like MIDI clock, a hardware interface box of some kind is required. Many of the modern multiport interfaces support SMPTE and MTC, which will be covered shortly.

SMPTE (pronounced 'simptee') is not directly related to MIDI in any way but is instead a sophisticated, real-time code system based on elapsed time rather than bars and beats, as in the case of MIDI clock. SMPTE is unnecessarily sophisticated for synchronising MIDI sequencers to tape machines, but if your model of sequencer has a dedicated, low-cost SMPTE sync unit available then it should take care of any unnecessary complications.

Why is SMPTE more complicated than MIDI clock? Because it is related to absolute time, rather than to relative tempo, it's rather like having an invisible ruler printed on your tape marking out hours, minutes, seconds and film frames. For example, the SMPTE readout for one hour, ten minutes, 30 seconds and eleven frames would appear thus: 01:10:30:11. Because there is no tempo information present in the time code itself a conversion has to be performed somewhere along the line, either by the computer running the sequencing software or by the micro-processor inside the SMPTE-to-MIDI sync box. To convert the SMPTE frame rate to tempo requires a bit of basic maths, but if you're lucky the sequencer software will be able to handle this for you quite automatically. If it can't do this you will have to key in a tempo map, which will inform the sync box or sequencer where the song starts, the tempo at which it runs and the location of any tempo changes. This is obviously tedious, especially if you compose music with lots of tempo changes. Fortunately, most modern software-based sequencers handle SMPTE synchronisation so easily that you only have to decide where the song starts. Some low-cost sequencer software, however, leaves out synchronisation facilities in order to save on cost.

SMPTE frames

Because of the different rates of film and TV frame used around the world, SMPTE comes in several frame formats. The most common is 30fps (feet per second) for US TV, 25fps for European TV and 24fps for film. Strictly speaking we should use the term SMPTE/EBU to cover all of the US and European formats, but most users abbreviate it to plain old SMPTE anyway. There's also a format called drop-frame which is used when converting one picture format to another, but this is rarely used for purely musical work and so will not be discussed here.

MTC

MTC (MIDI Time Code) follows the same format as SMPTE in that it is independent of musical tempo and expresses elapsed time in hours, minutes, seconds and frames, and all of the common SMPTE variants have an MTC equivalent. Standard MIDI clock sync doesn't include any position information, rather like the sprocket holes in cine film, and so if a sync pulse gets lost then the sequencer will happily follow along one pulse late. SMPTE, on the other hand, comprises a continuous stream of positional data, so if a short section of code gets lost or corrupted the system knows exactly where it's supposed to be the next time a piece of valid code is read.

MTC also includes positional information. However, because it has to share the MIDI data highway with other information, its data is sent in short bursts – four to each SMPTE frame. It takes eight of these quarter-frame messages to carry enough data to make up one complete set of location data, which means that the receiving MIDI device must read two frames of code before it knows where it's supposed to be. MTC technically can't pass on positional information as quickly or as accurately as SMPTE, but for practical applications using tape-to-MIDI sync some clever software developed by the sequencer designers ensures that there's no practical difference.

Some digital tape machines and many digital tapeless multitrack recorders can output MTC directly, which means that a sequencer can be synchronised without the use of any additional hardware, other than a MIDI cable.

MTC and timing

If MTC has a weakness it's that its position in the MIDI data stream can get jostled about when a lot of data is being sent. Therefore, if you have a multiport MIDI interface it's usually best to make sure that the port carrying the MTC signal isn't clogged with other MIDI data. If the MIDI data stream is running close to capacity then the MTC data may arrive a little behind schedule, which will have the effect of introducing a small amount of timing jitter. In really data-heavy situations this problem may be serious enough to become noticeable.

Fortunately, all of the major packages support MTC very effectively and take care of the hard work for you. Furthermore, all of the major sequencing packages handle it quite transparently, producing and storing a tempo map as part of the song file. To make use of MTC with a traditional tape recorder, a hardware sync box is required to convert the MTC MIDI signal into an FSK signal that can be recorded onto the tape.

striping tape

When using MTC or SMPTE, as opposed to MIDI clock, it's not necessary to create your sequence before recording the code onto tape. The MIDI clock-based FSK, on the other hand, requires that the sequence is programmed – at least in terms of length and tempo – before work is started. Furthermore, if you decide that a tempo change is in order you will then have to restripe with a new FSK code, whereas SMPTE or MTC simply require you to set up a new tempo map.

Before you can start working with SMPTE or MTC, the code must be recorded onto tape, a process known as striping. However, it's important to ensure that the correct frame rate is selected before this is done. Once the tape is striped, the sequencing software must be informed of a start time so that it knows where to begin playing in relation to the code on tape. Many SMPTE and MTC systems don't work reliably when crossing the 00:00:00:00 'midnight hour', so it's quite common, when striping the tape, to enter a time offset (one hour is an amount fairly easy to deal with) so that, when the tape is started a few seconds before the song begins, the code doesn't cross the midnight hour. Failure to observe this can result in a loss of sync or even a total freezing of the system. Once a SMPTE or MTC start time is selected, most sequencers automatically create a tempo map, which is then stored along with the song data when saved to disk. If the tempo is modified at any stage, the tempo map will be modified in turn the next time the song is saved.

key points to remember

* The master machine in a sync system must be set to Internal Sync mode, while any slaves should be set to External Sync.

* When a MIDI clock-based code is being recorded to tape the sequencer is the master, but when the code is played back the sequencer becomes the slave and must therefore be set to External MIDI Sync mode.

* With all MIDI clock-based sync systems it is impossible to vary the sequencer tempo once the code has been recorded to tape. Once the sequencer has been sync'ed up it will always play at the tempo of the code on the tape, regardless of any new changes.

* With SMPTE and MTC, the time code is striped onto the tape before the session starts. It's possible, when doing this, to stripe the entire tape with code in one go and then enter the appropriate start times for the various songs into the sequencer software.

- Because SMPTE/MTC carries only real, absolute information, a tempo map must be created so that the sequencer's tempo can be calculated from the real-time sync data. Most contemporary sequencing software packages manage this task automatically and save the tempo map as part of the song file.

- Be warned that analogue tape noise-reduction systems can cause sync codes to work unreliably. Dbx especially has difficulty in this respect, although Dolby is generally less problematic. Many cassette multitrackers have a dedicated synchronisation option which eliminates the noise reduction on the track onto which the code is being recorded, which is usually the track with the highest number. If no such facility is available, try setting the EQ to its flat position and experiment with different recording levels to find the one that provides the most reliable operation.

chapter 6

methods of synthesis

Synthesisers are fascinating instruments, able to produce a wide range of both imitative and abstract sounds. The character, or *timbre*, of a sound is determined by two key factors: the harmonics (and non-harmonic overtones) that make up that sound, and the changing of these components in both level and pitch as the sound evolves. The way in which the levels of the different harmonics and overtones change with time determines the envelope of the sound, and this evolution of the sound has a profound bearing on our interpretation of the sounds we hear. For example, a percussive sound has a very sharp, sudden attack, and the vibrations then die away because no new energy is being applied to sustain the sound. The sound of a bowed instrument such as a cello, on the other hand, may build up relatively slowly as the energy driving the sound is being applied over a period of time. When the driving energy is removed, in this case the bow, the string vibrations decay rapidly.

additive synthesis

To accurately synthesise a 'real' sound it would first be necessary to recreate all of the harmonics and overtones of the sound in question, then set their relative levels, then apply a separate envelope to each harmonic, and then vary the frequency of each to emulate the way in which they behave in real life. What's more, there would need to be some way of controlling the sound so that it changed in accordance with performing technique, exactly as a real instrument does.

Building a sound from scratch in this way is known as additive synthesis, and although technically possible it is extremely difficult to achieve in practice. Few practical synthesisers work on this principle.

analogue synthesis

Mainstream synthesis started with the analogue synthesiser, so called because it relies entirely on analogue circuitry, in which oscillators, filters and envelope shapers are controlled by electrical waveforms and voltages. Analogue circuitry doesn't possess the inherent stability of modern digital designs, and so parameters such as tuning tend to drift a little, especially if the room temperature changes significantly. However, the subtle detuning effects caused by this are thought to contribute to the warm, organic sound of analogue instruments. These days, although a few instruments are based on analogue circuitry, most attempt to emulate it by digital means.

The original analogue synths were monophonic and had no velocity sensitivity, so that notes were always produced at the same level, no matter how hard the keys were struck, and only one note could ever be produced at a time. Limited polyphony was later developed, but it's only in modern digital emulations that generous polyphony is possible.

subtractive synthesis

Subtractive synthesis is very much like sculpture, in that a large block of material is trimmed of anything that isn't needed. Analogue synthesis is a form of subtractive synthesis, as the process takes an harmonically rich sound and then uses filters to reduce the level of unwanted harmonics.

Analogue synthesis is akin to trying to create a sculpture using a clumsily-wielded shovel: the available tools aren't sufficiently refined to produce a work that captures the detail of real life. However, it allows interesting abstract sounds to be created in abundance.

sample and synthesis

Modern S&S (Sample and Synthesis) instruments also work on the subtractive principle, but instead of starting out with electronically-generated waveforms they use electronic samples (short recordings stored in microchips) of real instrumental sounds that are then further modified by filters and envelope shapers. The starting point for a modern S&S synth patch may be a sampled violin note, a flute, a piano or even a human voice, and some of these may then be looped, allowing them to be sustained indefinitely. Looped samples may be considered to be the equivalent of oscillators, because the sound they create continues to be generated for as long as the key is held. The samples used for short percussive sounds are generally not looped, however, and are allowed to decay naturally. Though digital, the processing architecture of S&S instruments is usually similar to that of analogue synthesisers.

FM synthesis

Originally popularised by Yamaha, FM synthesis relies on frequency-modulating oscillators which interact with other oscillators to produce harmonically-rich waveforms, a process accomplished entirely in the digital domain. The configurations by which the various oscillators are combined and modulated are called algorithms, and certain algorithms are best suited to producing certain types of sounds. Though not as intuitive as subtractive synthesis, using FM can be very effective for producing electronic piano, bell and bass sounds, as well as those of plucked instruments.

physical modelling

Instead of creating the sound using oscillators and filters, instruments which take physical modelling as their operational basis use sophisticated mathematical models to emulate the behaviour of real acoustic instruments. The simulation of a clarinet would involve simulating the vibration of the reed, the resonance of the tubular body of the instrument and the effect of the flared end of the tube. This is a very complicated technology, but the advantage is that the model of the instrument can be designed to behave just like the real thing. For example, the physical model of a flute might change its harmonic structure when played hard to make it sound like a real flute being overblown, while playing it quietly will result in more breath noise resonating in the tubular body.

Different mathematical models are required for different instruments, but it is possible to obtain convincing models of many acoustic instruments with this method. Various aspects of different instruments may even be combined to produce the sounds of instruments that don't exist in real life, and yet they will still respond like true instruments. For example, you could have the reed of a clarinet, the body of a flute and the bell of a trumpet, or you could create a double-sized sax. The number of user parameters in physical modelling is usually limited because of the complexity of the process, although some instruments have software-editing packages available for those people with the expertise and patience to design their own sounds.

soundcards

Until very recently soundcards had a reputation for producing a second-class quality of sound, but if you're prepared to spend a little more on one of the superior wavetable-based synth cards you can expect a sound that rivals that of a stand-alone synth. Also, because PC soundcards are purely software-driven devices, there is often a surprising amount of useful support software bundled in with the card, including sequencers, editor librarians, MIDI song files, mixer maps for the most commonly-used sequencers, and even sampling.

A typical multimedia soundcard will have one stereo audio input and one stereo audio output, thus allowing analogue audio to be recorded and played back. The card may also have a wavetable (sample and synthesis) synthesiser chip providing General MIDI sounds and effects, a joystick port that can double as MIDI In and Out ports, and even a sample player that can play .WAV sounds (the standard PC format for sound files). Both sounds and effects can normally be edited with the accompanying software. All soundcards come with a software driver, which is a small program that enables them to communicate with other programs, such as sequencers.

Many soundcards have RAM sockets on the board so that the sample RAM can be increased if desired. This simply enables the computer to play longer samples, or more samples at once. There will also most likely be audio input connections for a CD-ROM drive, on-board amplifiers for driving headphones or small desktop speakers, and a bundle of support software to make full use of the various facilities offered by the card, which will also include software drivers where appropriate. The more up-market cards may also offer digital input and output connectors (for interfacing with DAT machines or suitable CD players) and multiple audio inputs and/or outputs.

A basic PC MIDI music system will generally make use of the MIDI interface provided by the soundcard, and one of the most common working methods is to use a MIDI adaptor cable that plugs directly into the card's joystick port. Alternatively, you could buy a hardware adaptor, which may allow you to leave your joystick connected via a joystick Thru socket. These look like long multipin plugs with MIDI sockets built into them. However, I'm informed that some MIDI programs get upset if a joystick is left connected, so unplug it if in any doubt.

Unfortunately, simple one in/one out MIDI interfaces are limited in that you can only drive 16 external MIDI channels. With today's synth modules this usually means a single multitimbral instrument, but remember that internal soundcards (except possibly the daughterboard) use virtual MIDI ports. This is obviously good news if you're on a budget, as the internal soundcard sounds can be used at the same time as the external MIDI module and still only need one MIDI port.

If more ports are needed to handle additional external synths then a separate multiport MIDI interface will be required. A 'dumb' MIDI master keyboard can be simply connected to the MIDI In, while a MIDI synth would need to be set to Local Off so that the synth section could be driven from the MIDI Out port of the computer.

software synthesis

Software-based synthesis (that which uses the computer's own processing power, rather than hardware, to create sounds) is now becoming both affordable and respectable, especially now that today's computers have adequate computing power to run them, along with other audio functions. Once the domain of high-powered university computers, software synthesis is becoming more practical as computers continue to increase in power. Of course, these packages use up a considerable proportion of the computer's processing power and memory, depending on the sophistication of the software and how well it's written.

At the budget end of the market, systems that use software synthesis can rival budget soundcards for sound quality, and they are usually GM compatible. Their main application, however, is in the games market, and while they are very cheap and may be tempting, decent soundcards are now so affordable that it's probably better to pay a little extra for the real thing as in this way you'll maximise your processing power and probably enjoy better sounds. However, there are advanced software-synthesis systems that offer far more than mere emulations of cheap GM modules, and some of these are potentially very interesting. Check these out only once you've mastered your basic system.

samplers

At its most basic, a sampler is a synthesiser into which you can record your own sounds rather than being forced to use only those waveforms provided by the manufacturer. Once a sound has been recorded (into RAM memory) it can be played back at varying pitches, under the control of a MIDI keyboard or sequencer. To play a sample back at a higher pitch than its original the sampler has to speed up the sound, with the result that the sample also plays back faster. Conversely, if the pitch is lowered by slowing down the sample the sound will also increase in length. Because RAM memory only works when power is supplied, most samplers forget everything when they are switched off, which means that some form of permanent sound storage is required. Most samplers store information on floppy disks, but some of the more serious models also offer the option of hard-disk storage.

Library sounds are also available on CD-ROMs, which may be loaded directly into those samplers equipped with a CD-ROM drive.

It is helpful at this stage to examine the two most common ways in which people use samplers. If single musical notes are sampled, such as strings or organ sounds, then the sampler can be played much like any other synthesiser. For the sampled sound to be musically useful, the sampler needs to work polyphonically so that chords can be played. As with synths there is a limit to the available polyphony, and most modern machines are also multitimbral in a similar manner to conventional synths.

Another popular way of using samplers is to use them to record whole musical or rhythmic phrases rather than just individual notes, and this way of working forms the cornerstone of the construction of modern dance music. A typical application might be to sample a four-bar drum rhythm and then trigger this on the first beat of every bar to provide a continuous rhythmic backing.

Because sampled sounds are held in RAM, the maximum sampling time available to you is always limited by the amount of memory available to the computer. A fully-expanded, top-of-the-range sampler may be able to hold several minutes' worth of samples, so it's therefore probably worth fitting as much RAM to your computer as you can afford.

As with synthesisers, sustained waveforms are often looped to conserve sample memory. Most sustained sounds have a distinctive attack portion, but after this the sound becomes more consistent as they start to decay. If this is the case, you can often sample just the first few seconds of the sound and then use the sampler's editing facilities to create a loop so that the middle part of the sample repeats itself continually after the key has been released. The level envelope shaper may then be used to recreate the natural decay of the sound.

If a sampled piano sounds natural for only a couple of semitones either side of its original pitch, the only way to maintain a natural sound is to take several samples of the original instrument at different pitches and use each sample over a limited part of the keyboard. This process is known as multisampling, and the zones of the keyboard covered by each sample are known as keygroups. The more keygroups that are available the more accurate the resulting sound will be, but this will also require more memory to hold all of the samples.

envelopes

With both samplers and traditional synthesisers, the raw sound of the source sample is usually passed through a filter and a level envelope shaper. The

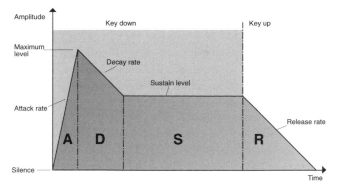

Figure 6.1: ADSR envelope shaper

character of a natural sound is largely determined by its harmonic content and the nature of its envelope, where the envelope is determined as the way in which the level of the sound changes with time. Percussive sounds start suddenly and then die away, whereas a bowed sound might start quite slowly and then sustain at a more or less fixed level. The envelopes of real sounds can be very complex, but an adequate approximation can often be achieved using a basic, four-stage ADSR (Attack, Decay, Sustain, Release) envelope generator controlling a VCA (Voltage-Controlled Amplifier). An ADSR envelope is shown in Figure 6.1. The envelope shaper is triggered by the pressing of a key.

The attack portion of the envelope is the time taken for the amplitude to reach its maximum level, so for percussive sounds the attack time should be as short as possible. Once the sound has reached its maximum level it then starts to decay at a rate set by the decay time setting, until it reaches a level known as the sustain level (another user-variable parameter). It remains at this level for as long as the key is held down, but once it is released the sound then resumes its decay, this time at a new rate determined by the release setting. If a new key is depressed before the envelope generator has completed its release phase, the old release is abandoned and a new envelope is initiated. This type of envelope generator, and more complex variations of it, are regularly found in modern digital synthesisers. It is important to note that, while attack, decay and release control the rate at which the envelope settings change, the sustain parameter is a level, not a rate.

filtering

Although some very basic modern synths dispense with the filter altogether, using instead ready-filtered sounds within their menu of basic waveforms, a filter is very useful in creating new or moving timbres. To achieve this a filter is required, the characteristics of which can be varied in a controllable way, and an envelope generator must be used to control the rate at which the filter frequency increases and decreases.

Like oscillators, filters may be controlled from a keyboard (on which the higher the note you play the higher the filter frequency), from an envelope generator or from an LFO, resulting in a filter characteristic that varies rather than remaining static. Cheaper synths tend to share the same envelope generator for both filter and output level, while more sophisticated models have separate envelope generators for each function.

polyphony

The polyphony of an instrument determines the number of different notes it can play at the same time. Digital synthesisers usually have 64- or even 128-note polyphony, and with multitimbral instruments this polyphony is shared between all parts. Sometimes there is a system for sharing out the polyphony so that each part always has one or two voices in reserve and aren't robbed by a rush of activity in other parts.

on-board effects

It is now common practise for synthesisers to come complete with built-in digital effects, such as reverb, chorus and echo/delay, to add life and realism to a performance. There is usually a choice of effect types or combinations, and it is possible for users inclined to do so to edit the effect and change the features such as reverb decay time, echo decay time and so on. The way in which the effects can be deployed when the synth is used multitimbrally varies from manufacturer to manufacturer, but it's pretty common for the key aspects of the effects to be MIDI controllable. For example, on GM instruments the level of chorus and reverb effects may be varied from part to part.

performance control

The secret of a convincing performance on any synthesiser is to make full use of real-time control, including (but not limited to) pitch bend and vibrato. For example, it's possible to use the modulation wheel to add both vibrato and tremolo simultaneously, while the pitch-bend wheel could similarly be set up not only to change pitch but also to cause a timbral change by linking it to the filter cut-off frequency.

Pedals are also practical, but not all keyboards are designed to accept a pedal input. Aftertouch can be a useful performance control and comes built into many keyboards, though it tends to act universally on all of the notes which are being played. As mentioned earlier, because aftertouch generates a lot of data it's a good idea to switch it off at the keyboard if you're not using it.

Joysticks are also fitted to some instruments, and these are useful devices in that they can control two parameters at a time, one vertically and one horizontally. These can often be assigned to any of the regular MIDI controllers, which means that you can decide on those parameters that they will affect.

Ribbon controllers are rarely fitted to modern instruments, but they seem to be making a bit of a comeback in some circles. A ribbon controller is a flat ribbon beneath which is a conductive strip, and so when the ribbon is pressed down it makes an electrical contact. As you slide your finger from one end of the ribbon to the other the electrical resistance of the contact changes, just as it would with a normal slider, and so any function can be dynamically controlled. Unlike a slider, however, as soon as you remove your finger from the ribbon the contact is broken and the original setting is restored. Ribbons are useful for controlling such things as level, pitch, vibrato, filter brightness and so on.

Breath controllers are also relatively rare now, and if you want to use one you'll probably either need to buy a third-party breath-control interface box or use a synth module that has its own breath-control input. The controller itself is a headset attached to a simple mouthpiece, into which the performer blows. A pressure sensor converts breath pressure to electrical information, which is subsequently used to generate MIDI controller data. Anything that can be controlled via a MIDI controller can also be controlled via a breath-control unit, although most people set them to controller seven (master volume) to achieve overall control of the volume.

software editors

Because most modern synths employ a menu-and-button-driven user interface, it is often easier to edit them on a computer screen where several parameters can be seen and adjusted at once. Level and filter envelopes may also be presented graphically, with facilities available for dragging them into new shapes. This allows a more intuitive style of editing, but buying a software editor for each instrument you own can end up being expensive.

Universal synth editors adopt a modular approach, whereby software modules relating to the various synths in circulation can be loaded in and used. Such a software system may initially be more expensive than a single synth editor, but the advantage is that you then have the ability to edit dozens of different models and makes of instrument.

Editing systems usually include librarian facilities so that, if your synth memory fills up with new sounds, you can then store them on disk. In this way you can build up a vast library of different sounds for various instruments and then transfer these to your synthesisers as they're needed.

To use an editor/librarian system it is first necessary to connect the MIDI Out of the instrument being edited to the MIDI In of the interface serving the computer, and the MIDI Out of the interface must in turn be connected back to the MIDI In of the instrument. This setup allows two-way communication between the instrument and the computer so that patch data and instructions can be sent both ways. Figure 6.2 shows the MIDI connection necessary for editing.

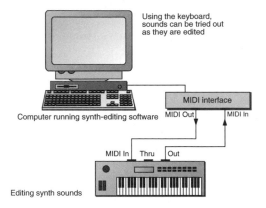

Using the keyboard, sounds can be tried out as they are edited

Computer running synth-editing software

Editing synth sounds

Figure 6.2: Connecting a MIDI editor

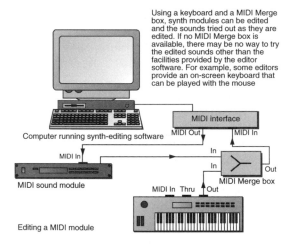

Using a keyboard and a MIDI Merge box, synth modules can be edited and the sounds tried out as they are edited. If no MIDI Merge box is available, there may be no way to try the edited sounds other than the facilities provided by the editor software. For example, some editors provide an on-screen keyboard that can be played with the mouse

Computer running synth-editing software

MIDI sound module

MIDI Merge box

Editing a MIDI module

alternative MIDI instruments

The marriage of MIDI and keyboards is one made in heaven: electronic circuitry likes the certainty of switches, and a MIDI keyboard is really just a row of switches. However, not every musician plays a keyboard, and various instruments have been manufactured or adapted to generate MIDI information, including (but not limited to) guitars, violins, wind instruments, drums and even accordions. The electric guitar is still the most popular contemporary instrument so I'll tackle that first.

guitars and MIDI

Guitars don't lend themselves naturally to MIDI because, unlike the electronic keyboard, the notes are created by vibrating strings rather than by turning oscillators on or off with switches. In order to generate MIDI information there has to be some means of measuring the pitch of each string, but the signal from a conventional guitar pickup is too complex to analyse if more than one string is sounding at a time. The most common solution is to use a split pickup – in effect one pickup per string – so that each string can be monitored independently of its neighbours. Once a note is played, a specially-designed circuit measures the frequency of the note generated and sends it to a small processor, which then generates the required MIDI data.

It sounds simple, but because of the harmonic complexity of a plucked guitar string accidental mistracking occasionally plagues even the most advanced systems. To compound these difficulties, there's also no 'key-up' event to inform the processor when the note has ended, so if the player doesn't terminate the note by damping or lifting off a finger there's no telling when the note will stop – it all depends on the sustain of the guitar. And just that action of removing a finger from a string can cause the open string to vibrate just enough to cause an accidental retrigger. However, as a MIDI sequencer provides you with the opportunity to fix mistakes afterwards, the guitar can be a practical way of recording MIDI information.

MIDI mono mode

To enable each string of a guitar to be used for independent note bends in a MIDI setup, each string must be handled by a different MIDI channel. The most authentic results can be achieved by using a synth that can work in MIDI mode four, which in effect puts each guitar string in control of its own part of a multitimbral module and allows each part to play only monophonically. After all, a guitar string can only play one note at a time.

Even when there is no intention to bend notes, it is essential to stick with the one channel, one string approach if hammer-ons and slides are to be tracked accurately. These are occasions when it can be advantageous to simply plug the guitar synth into a module set to Poly mode. Even though bends, hammers and slides can't be used in this situation, this mode provides a reasonably reliable way of triggering simple parts, such as block chords or straight melody lines.

MIDI violins

MIDI violins usually work on a similar principle to MIDI guitars, in that they have a separate pickup for each string, but as violins don't use metal strings the pickups are more likely to be piezo-electric devices. Because of the possible interference that the noise of the bow can cause to the tracking process, ingenious multiple-pickup systems are sometimes employed in an attempt to cancel it out, and elaborate electronic filtering is used to strip away harmonics so that the fundamental frequency is easier to detect.

wind controllers

Various wind controller have been built over time, most most of which have relied on switches or touch sensors to duplicate the functions of the keys on a clarinet or similar instrument. These switches provide the note information in a similar manner to that of the keys on a regular keyboard, and a special mouthpiece capable of measuring breath pressure and lip pressure provides additional controller information, which has the effect of adding more life to the sound. The instruments may also be fitted with sliders, modulation wheels or ribbon controllers that the player can operate with his thumb, along with other refinements such as octave switches.

Played well the wind controller is a most impressive instrument, and used in combination with one of the newer physical-modelling synths the overall sound has a stunning realism. Like real wind instruments these controllers are monophonic, though you can still set your synth to play parallel intervals, such as fourths, fifths and octaves.

drum controllers

MIDI drum systems have been around for many years because they're not to difficult to design, compared to other controller systems. Usually a synthetic rubber pad is used instead of a drumhead, which is then fitted with a special pickup that monitors how hard the pad has been struck. All hits are converted by a processor into MIDI Note On and Off messages of differing velocities, depending on how hard the pad has been struck.

A separate floor-mounted pad is often used in conjunction with a conventional bass drum pedal for producing bass drum sounds, and a regular footswitch often serves as a simple hi-hat open/close switch. The sounds of hi-hats and other cymbals are usually triggered by the same types of pads as those triggering the sounds of the drums, though some of the more sophisticated systems use pads with position sensors which allow two MIDI-controlled sounds to be cross-faded as the player plays across the surface of the pad. For example, a cymbal might have the sounds of a cymbal bell near the centre and a ride cymbal near the edge.

drum pads

Drum pads may be available on fully-sized pads to replace the conventional drum kit, or they may be presented as a number of smaller pads fitted to the surface of a unit no larger than a briefcase. This latter type is more practical for use in the home MIDI studio, and most varieties have inputs to accept pedals and bass drum pads.

The most advanced pad systems allow the user to send out sequences of notes from specific pads, either in programmed or random order, and if these are assigned to slightly different cymbal sounds, for example, then the sound will change with every hit, thus resulting in a more natural sound. The same trick can be used to make snare drum rolls sound more natural.

chapter 7

practical sequencing

When you finally start to put the techniques you've learned this far into practise, the first thing you should do is make sure you have a comfortable working position. Sitting at a badly-positioned computer for any length of time soon results in back ache, neck ache and wrist ache, none of which help in the creative process of writing music. You'll also need to be able to get at your music keyboard, and of course you'll need to be comfortably positioned relative to that, too.

sequencer familiarisation

MIDI sequencing starts at the keyboard, which is connected via its MIDI Out to the MIDI In of your MIDI interface or soundcard. (If you have an Atari ST, the interface is built into the computer itself). If your keyboard includes a synth section, rather than being just a dumb master keyboard, then switch to Local Off and plug a MIDI cable from the sequencer's MIDI Out to the keyboard's MIDI In. If you have other MIDI modules in the system you can daisy chain them in any order by feeding the MIDI Thru of one piece of equipment to the MIDI In of the next module in the chain.

If you haven't used a computer before, take some time to read the manual and then try a few exercises to get used to the mouse. Ensure that you know how to start the machine and how to shut it down properly – you don't just pull out the mains plug when you're done! You'll also need to know how to format and use floppy disks, how to open and close files, and if you're using a Mac or a PC you'll also need to know how to open, close and move windows. Only when you're happy with your computer's basic operations should you attempt any sequencing.

the arrange page

Though every sequencer package on the market has a slightly different user interface, most of the successful examples bear more than a passing resemblance to Steinberg's Cubase, in which the main page shows the sequencer tracks running from left to right across the screen. Hardware sequencers tend to be a little less consistent, but the basic principles of selecting and recording tracks, playing back sequences and editing are roughly comparable. The arrange page of a typical sequencer is shown in Figure 7.1.

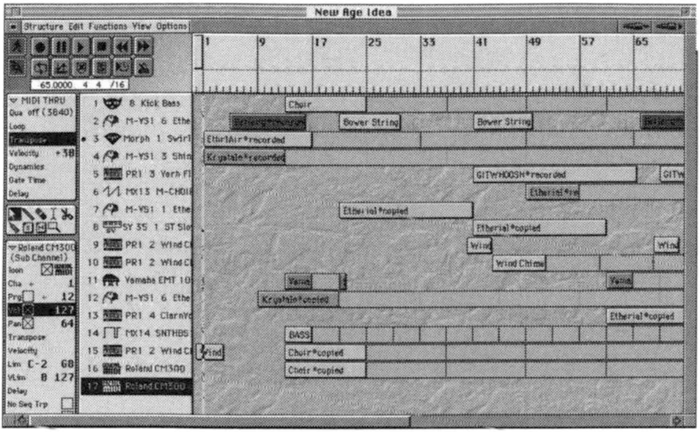

Figure 7.1: Arrange page of a typical software sequencer

Each track can be set to record on any MIDI channel, so you don't have to use track one for MIDI channel one. To start with, however, it might be less confusing to set up track one to channel one, track two to channel two and so on. If a multiport interface is fitted you'll get a choice of 16 channels on (for example) MIDI ports A, B, C and so on.

program selection

Having set your tracks to the MIDI channels you wish to use, you should then enter a MIDI program-change number for each track, which will force your synth module or soundcard to play the sound program of your choice. Most GM soundcards can have their patch names displayed within the arrange page of the sequencer, which makes choosing sounds fairly straightforward. If yours doesn't, you'll need to open your synth's manual to the page showing the patch chart so that you can see the number which corresponds to the sound you want, unless you have a sequencer package that allows you to type in the patch names of all of your synths. This may be tedious at first, but you'll be thankful of it later when you can call every synth patch up by name rather than by number. If you have to work using program numbers, it helps to have a photocopy of the General MIDI patch list pinned to the wall. Keep your sequencer manual handy so that you can find out exactly how the various functions are accessed in your software.

tempo

Now set the tempo to suit the music you wish to record. You can always change the tempo after recording, so if you're not a great player you may want to set this slightly slower than it would be in real time to make recording easier. When you start recording the computer will play a simple metronome click, either via the speaker or via your MIDI drum sounds. After a short count in, the selected track will record everything you play into it. I find click tracks very limiting to play against, so I usually record a simple drum pattern first and use this as the metronome.

drumming made easy

If you find it difficult to play drum parts, here's a tip: create three or four sequencer tracks, all set to the channel of your drum sounds (usually channel ten), and record your drum part in layers. First put the bass drum part on one track, and then, when this is OK, record the snare drum part in isolation on the next drum track. When these are both working together, record your hi-hat part. It sometimes helps if you actually drum on the keys with your two forefingers rather than trying to play the drum rhythms as you would the rhythm of a regular piano part. If you don't know which keys represent which drum sounds, refer to the drum map in your sequencer manual and consider sticking labels on the keys corresponding to the drum sounds you want to use.

Most sequencers have a facility for merging the data on different tracks – Cubase and similarly-styled programs use an icon in the tool palette resembling a tube of glue to combine the data from selected tracks into a single track.

copy and loop

You obviously don't want to have to tap out the guide drum rhythm for the whole length of the song, so your best bet is to create just one or two bars, and then copy that part as many times as is needed. Some sequencers, such as Logic, allow you to loop sections so that they play indefinitely, while other programs have a copy menu which will allow you to enter the number of copies you want.

the next track

Once your guide drum part is tapping away happily, choose a new track and play whichever keyboard part is most appropriate. You can turn the original metronome click down or off if it's distracting you, as you now have a drum part to follow.

Once you've recorded two or three tracks, listen to your performance to check the timing. If you're a good player then you'll almost certainly have more 'feel' in your performance by not quantising it, but if you're a bit on the sloppy side it may need tightening up. Before you dive straight for the quantise button, however, make sure that your sequencer supports percentage quantise. Most good sequencer have this facility, and the idea is that, if you set, say, 50%

quantise, the note you've played will be shifted so that it falls halfway between where you played it and where the computer thinks it ought to be. The higher the percentage you set the further the note moves towards the rigid quantise value. By choosing the right percentage you can tighten up your performance and still leave a degree of human feel in it.

moving your music

Another very powerful feature of sequencers is the ability to move data around. For example, you may have put together a composition but now you have decided that the synth solo should start a couple of bars later. This is no problem if you're using Cubase or one of those packages with a similar interface because all you have to do is drag the sequence to a new position with the mouse. What's more, if you want to copy it to a new position without changing the original there's usually a keyboard modifier whereby you can hold down a key and then drag a copy to its new location. Once again the key commands vary from package to package, so check your manual. This technique is invaluable for copying repeated sections such as verses or choruses, as you only have to record each section once, after which you can drag copies around to experiment with alternative arrangements.

divide and conquer

Before leaving this section, I should mention the knife or scissors tool usually found in the tool palette. This is provided so that you can cut up a recorded sequence into two or more parts. You may simply want to divide an eight-bar section into two four-bar sections so that you can copy or move the individual parts, but you can also use it, for example, to chop up an improvised solo into shorter sections so that you can assemble only those parts that worked. Though there is a lot of similarity between leading sequencer software packages, the tool palettes tend to differ slightly. Ensure that you're aware what all the tools are for and practice using them.

more on editing

At this stage in the proceedings the idea is to become familiarised with the sequencer rather than record a hit single. Therefore, instead of trying to perfect that solo synth part, let's move on to explore some of the editing tricks that can be performed on the data you've just recorded.

Find the transpose option and move the melody part up or down an octave and hear how that sounds. Transpose is very handy if you want to create a part that's outside the range of your keyboard, but you might also find that the part you've recorded simply sounds better when played back an octave higher or lower. A useful trick is to copy the data from one track to an empty track set to a different MIDI channel, set it to a different sound and then raise it or drop it by an octave. You will then have two different instruments playing back the same part but an octave apart.

grid edit

The other editing process with which you should familiarise yourself is the fixing of wrong notes. Once again, most sequencer packages have a grid-edit window of some kind, in which the notes are represented as bars on a grid depicting time (in beats and bars) in one direction and pitch (in semitones) in the other. This is sometimes called a 'piano-roll editor', as a piano-keyboard graphic is used to depict the pitch axis of the grid. Figure 7.2 shows the grid-edit page from a popular sequencing package. To correct wrong notes it is necessary only to drag them with the mouse until they at the right pitch or the right timing position on the grid.

MIDI event list

If you're not comfortable with grid editing then you should investigate the MIDI event list, which represents

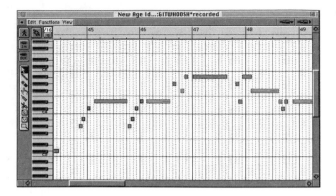

Figure 7.2: Grid-edit page from a popular sequencing package

your composition as a long list of MIDI events, each marked with its beat and bar location. Values in this list may be changed. Figure 7.3 shows the edit list from a typical sequencing package.

score edit

Finally, the musically literate may prefer to edit notes on the stave, and most serious sequencer software allows this. Notes may be physically dragged to new pitches, deleted or inserted, and some of the more advanced packages allow you to prepare a full multipart score on the screen, ready for printing.

Figure 7.4 shows the score-edit window used by a typical sequencing package.

Once you've finished writing your song and you've done any editing that needs to be done, it's important not to forget to save your song before switching the computer off, or all of your work will be lost.

POSITION				STATUS	CHA	NUM	VAL	LENGTH/INFO			
----	----	----	----	Start of List	----	----	----				
21	1	1	1	NOTE	1	B1	25	3	3	1	220
21	1	1	1	NOTE	1	E2	32	3	3	1	216
21	1	1	1	NOTE	1	G#2	12	3	3	1	80
21	1	1	1	NOTE	1	C#3	17	3	3	1	168
21	1	1	1	NOTE	1	D#3	18	3	3	1	60
25	1	1	1	NOTE	1	G#1	103	3	3	3	232
25	1	1	1	NOTE	1	E2	103	3	3	3	232
25	1	1	1	NOTE	1	G#2	103	3	3	3	232
25	1	1	1	NOTE	1	D#3	103	3	3	3	232
25	1	1	1	NOTE	1	G#3	103	3	3	3	232
29	1	1	1	NOTE	1	F#1	97	3	3	3	52
29	1	1	1	NOTE	1	D#2	97	3	3	3	52
29	1	1	1	NOTE	1	C#3	97	3	3	3	52
33	1	1	1	NOTE	1	G#1	97	3	3	3	52
33	1	1	1	NOTE	1	C#2	97	3	3	3	52
33	1	1	1	NOTE	1	A#2	97	3	3	3	52
37	1	1	1	NOTE	1	B1	97	3	3	3	52
37	1	1	1	NOTE	1	E2	97	3	3	3	52
37	1	1	1	NOTE	1	G#2	97	3	3	3	52
37	1	1	1	NOTE	1	C#3	97	3	3	3	52
37	1	1	1	NOTE	1	B3	97	3	3	3	52
----	----	End of List	----								

Figure 7.3: MIDI edit list

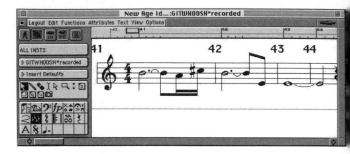

Figure 7.4: Score-edit window

more features

What has been described this far represents only a small proportion of what a powerful sequencer package is capable, but once the basic recording and editing skills that have been discussed so far have been mastered you should know enough to start making serious use of your sequencer. Most of the time you will probably only need to use a fraction of your sequencer's features – you can explore the more sophisticated features as and when you feel that you need them. However, it's inevitable that you will come up against the occasional difficulty, so to this end I've listed some of the more common problems and their solutions.

troubleshooting

- Double-check your MIDI cable connections: you may have a faulty MIDI lead or you may be plugged into a MIDI Out when you meant to connect to a MIDI In. Most sequencers have an on-screen indication that they're receiving MIDI data, while many modules have an LED or other indicator that lets you know that data is being received.

- If two or more instruments try to play the same part, the chances are that you've either got more than one module set to the same MIDI channel or something has been left set to Omni.

- If your master keyboard plays its own sounds when you're trying to record using the sound of another module, make sure that Local Off is really set to Off. On some instruments, Local status defaults to Local On every time you switch on the machine.

- If you experience stuck notes, apparently limited polyphony or rapidly repeating notes, this may be due to a MIDI loop. In a MIDI loop, MIDI data passes through the sequencer, through the MIDI input of the master keyboard, and then starts its round trip all over again, rather like acoustic feedback. Once again, the most common cause is the setting of the master keyboard's Local status to Local On when it should be set to Local Off.

If you have an older keyboard with no Local Off mode, disable the MIDI Thru function on whichever channel your master keyboard is transmitting. Check your sequencer manual to find out how to do this.

- If the sequencer records OK but plays back the wrong sound then this could be because you have forgotten to enter a MIDI program-change number into your sequencer track. It can also happen when you loop a section of MIDI data that has a Program Change command embedded into it.

saving your song

Save your song every few minutes, just in case there's a crash, and make floppy backups in case your hard drive crashes one day. Most sequencers will also allow you the option of saving your work in Standard MIDI file format so that your work can be freely swapped between different types of sequencer. Commercially-available song files are invariably in Standard MIDI file format, usually on PC-formatted disks. Atari ST computers can read Standard MIDI files from PC disks, while Apple Macs need to have either System 7.5 running or a PC-to-Mac utility program such as AccessPC.

automating MIDI

This next section is just a little more advanced, so if you don't feel like trying it out yet, that's fine. However, it's easier to do than to read about, and I'm sure you'll find that it opens up many interesting possibilities.

As you've learned already, MIDI controllers can be used to adjust many different parameters relating to a musical instrument. The most useful in a mix situation are main volume (controller seven) and pan (controller ten), but you aren't limited to automating volume and pan during a mix – in theory you can change any parameter of an instrument that is assignable to a MIDI controller, including portamento rate (controller five), sustain pedal (controller 64) and, where supported, things like filter frequency or resonance. These latter parameters aren't defined controllers and so it's up to individual manufacturers if and how they are implemented. In this case you'll have to look in the back of the instrument manual to see exactly what you can access via MIDI. It really is worth looking into those apparently tedious back pages once in a while.

practical MIDI automation

When it comes to using controller information to set up volume and pan effects you will first have to make sure that your instruments respond to these messages. This may sound obvious, but there are a few older instruments out there that are totally oblivious even to master volume, set at controller seven. The only way to fade one of these is either to pull down the fader by hand or to doctor the MIDI note velocity data in your sequencer's MIDI event list so that the notes actually become quieter.

Thanks to modern sequencer design there are now many ways to enter controller information. In the early days you had to add controller numbers and values to the MIDI event list or record them in real time, but now there are often more intuitive graphic methods. If you have a keyboard with assignable data sliders or wheels then you have an even more convenient way of sending controller data, in real time, without having to edit it afterwards. Some computer-based sequencers allow you to create on-screen faders that can be moved with the mouse or with the keyboard, and if there are functions you use regularly it's best to save these as part of your default song so that you don't need to re-invent the wheel every time you start to write a new tune.

When automating areas like level and pan using controller data you must remember that, if you insert a fade-out at the end of a song, the next time you run the song those instruments you have faded out will still remain turned down until new controller information is sent. That being the case, don't just use controller data to fade the last few seconds of your song but also set your controller data at the beginning of the song, during the count-in bar, to set your starting levels. The same is true of pan: if everything goes out stage left it will stay there until either the instrument is reset or new controller information is registered. It's a good habit to set your controller information at the start of each song, and once again you can record this in the template for your default song so that you only have to do it once. You can always make any required changes once the song is loaded.

Because it's so easy to automate instruments in a MIDI mix you'll probably find that you are able to do things of which you hadn't previously been capable, and though you may go over the top at first don't be reluctant to experiment – it's only because users have constantly pushed at the boundaries of MIDI's capabilities that we have such a powerful MIDI specification available to us today. All of your automation data will be saved with your song, so you can recreate the same mix exactly any time.

transferring sequencer files

Standard MIDI song files have already been introduced as a method of transferring data from one sequencer to another, and despite their limitations they can work extremely well. In fact there are three different types of MIDI file: format 0, on which the entire song is saved as a single sequencer track; format one, on which the sequencer tracks are kept separate; and format two, on which the song is saved as a series of patterns. Format one is probably the most useful, and it is the most commonly encountered. However, when you load up a format one MIDI file you may find that the tracks don't come up with their original MIDI channel numbers, and sometimes they also lose their names. This depends on how the sequencer which created the data stores its information, and restoring order is usually fairly straightforward. It must be noted, however, that standard MIDI files don't convey MIDI port information, and can only be used to store a maximum of 16 different MIDI channels.

If you need to transfer a file to or from a hardware sequencer or a non-standard computer platform you may find that the disk formats are completely incompatible, in which case it may be necessary to transfer files by playing them out of one sequencer and recording them into another. However, there is slightly

more to this than meets the eye, and for this process to
to work properly you should proceed as follows.

• Connect the two sequencers together with MIDI
  leads so that the MIDI Out of each machine feeds
  into the MIDI In of the other. This two-way
  connection is necessary to ensure accurate timing
  of the transferred information.

• Set the sequencer containing the song you want to
  copy to External Sync mode. It must be clocked by
  the receiving device to ensure optimum accuracy of
  timing. Leave the receiving sequencer set to
  Internal Sync mode. If the receiving device has a
  'soft' MIDI Thru function, switch this off to
  minimise the amount of data sharing the MIDI Out
  with the timing clock.

• Set the receiving sequencer to record MIDI data but
  choose a slow tempo, again to maintain optimum
  timing accuracy. The reason timing accuracy is so
  important is that all of the data for all of the tracks
  is being recorded at once, and sequencers are
  better at outputting lots of tracks than they are at
  receiving them. A tempo of around 50 beats per
  minute should be fine. This can be set to the correct
  value once you've captured the data.

- Start the receiving sequencer recording and the transmitting sequencer will automatically start and run in sync with it.

- If you still find that the timing is inaccurate, repeat the procedure with all of the tracks from the source sequencer muted except for one. In this way you can send one track at a time. When the recording is complete, select a new source track and a new destination track and repeat the procedure until all of the tracks have been recorded. This procedure is a trifle slow and tedious, but if the song is important then the effort will be worth it.

tidying up

Finally, if you were able to transfer all of the data in one go you'll find that your whole song occupies a single track in the destination sequencer. Most modern sequencers have a 'de-merge by MIDI channel' function, and this will automatically sort the data out into separate tracks based on their MIDI channel numbers. You will probably still need to pair up each part with the instrument playing it, but if the original file contained program information this should have come over as well. If you don't have this function then you can look forward to picking through the data manually, which is

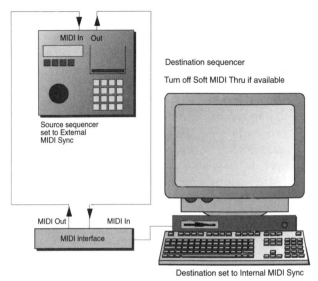

Figure 7.5: Sequencer-to-sequencer transfer

a very time-consuming process. One way to do this
would be to copy the song track to all 16 tracks and then
edit one track at a time, discarding any data on the MIDI
channel not appropriate to that track. In this way you'll
end up with all MIDI channel one data on track one,
channel two data on track two and so on. Figure 7.5
shows how two sequencers are connected for data
transfer in this way.

user tips

- Create a default song, an empty song file that has your instruments already set up and ready to go. Store a copy on a locked floppy disk, or as a locked file on your hard drive, so that it can't be overwritten by accident. A typical default song will contain the MIDI channel and track assignment for your different instruments, suitable 'vanilla' starting patches, any user options the software might provide and various MIDI status functions such as MIDI Thru, MIDI click and so on.

- Create your own metronome. Rather than using the default metronome when recording, program a simple drum part to work against. As well as providing you with a better feel, you'll also find it easier to keep time against. It will also pay you to save your guide percussion parts, either in a separate song or as a part of your default song. This way they'll always be available whenever you start a new song.

- Use your computer keyboard. Although most jobs can be tackled using the mouse, some things are faster and easier with the keyboard.

- Copy important documentation. The trouble with most MIDI systems is that you end up with a stack of manuals a foot thick. It helps enormously to photocopy the preset patch lists for all of your instruments, and also to type out the names and descriptions of your user patches and contents of your memory card. These sheets may then be put into plastic sleeves and clipped into a single binder or pinned to the wall.

- Use custom screens. Some programs, such as Notator Logic, have a built-in system for saving and accessing various screen layouts. If you're using a program where you need several windows to be open at once then this facility can be a real time saver, as a single keystroke can bring up a screen layout you have previously specified with all of the windows at the proper dimensions and in exactly the right place.

- Don't over-quantise. Those who criticise electronic music for its robotic sound have probably heard the result of too much quantising. It's true that some forms of music demand a rigid, mechanical approach to timing, but if you want to keep the feel of the original performance it may be better not to quantise at all and just use the sequencer as you would a tape recorder. If you feel that your playing needs to be tightened up but you don't want it to sound lifeless, try the percentage quantise function.

- Playing 'free'. If you have a part that needs to be played free (without reference to any specific tempo), simply turn down the click track, turn off all quantisation and record the part just as if you were playing it into a tape recorder.

- Back up your work. In fact, be paranoid about backing up. Computers have a habit of crashing or locking up when you least expect them to, so save every few minutes. When working with a hard drive, back up important work onto floppies at the end of each session. Modern drives are reliable but not infallible.

- Keep a notebook. Paper may be a low-tech commodity, but when you come across a six-month-old disk filled with MIDI files named something like 'Ideas 1-99', a few notes can be worth their weight in gold.

- If you create your own MIDI control data for cyclic panning, or if you have an assortment of killer drum fills, hoard them. Create your own MIDI equivalent of clip art so that, instead of always having to work from scratch, you can copy and paste various useful odds and ends from a library file.

common cable connections

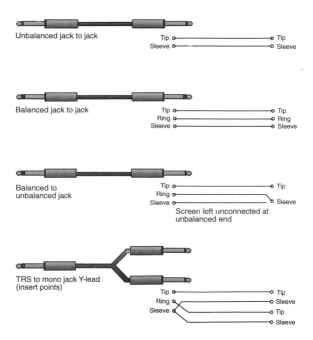

Unbalanced jack to jack

Tip o————————o Tip
Sleeve o————————o Sleeve

Balanced jack to jack

Tip o————————o Tip
Ring o————————o Ring
Sleeve o————————o Sleeve

Balanced to unbalanced jack

Tip o————————o Tip
Ring o————————o
Sleeve o————————o Sleeve

Screen left unconnected at unbalanced end

TRS to mono jack Y-lead (insert points)

Tip o————————o Tip
Ring o————————o Sleeve
Sleeve o————————o Tip
————————o Sleeve

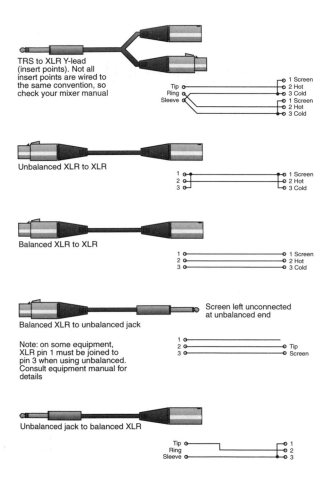

TRS to XLR Y-lead
(insert points). Not all
insert points are wired to
the same convention, so
check your mixer manual

Tip / Ring / Sleeve → 1 Screen / 2 Hot / 3 Cold / 1 Screen / 2 Hot / 3 Cold

Unbalanced XLR to XLR

1 / 2 / 3 → 1 Screen / 2 Hot / 3 Cold

Balanced XLR to XLR

1 / 2 / 3 → 1 Screen / 2 Hot / 3 Cold

Balanced XLR to unbalanced jack

Screen left unconnected
at unbalanced end

Note: on some equipment,
XLR pin 1 must be joined to
pin 3 when using unbalanced.
Consult equipment manual for
details

1 / 2 / 3 → Tip / Screen

Unbalanced jack to balanced XLR

Tip / Ring / Sleeve → 1 / 2 / 3

glossary

active

Circuit containing transistors, ICs, tubes and other devices that require power to operate and are capable of amplification.

active sensing

System used to verify that a MIDI connection is working, in which the sending device frequently sends short messages to the receiving device to reassure it that all is well. If these active sensing messages stop for any reason, the receiving device will recognise a fault condition and switch off all notes. Not all MIDI devices support active sensing.

ADSR

Envelope generator with Attack, Decay, Sustain and Release parameters. This is a simple type of envelope generator and was first used on early analogue synthesisers, though similar envelopes may be found in some effects units to control filter sweeps and suchlike.

AFL

After-Fade Listen, a system used within mixing consoles to allow specific signals to be monitored at the level set by their fader or level control knob. Aux sends are generally monitored AFL rather than PFL so that the actual signal being fed to an be monitored.

,h

,enerating a control signal based on how much
is applied to the keys of a MIDI keyboard. Most
nts that support this do not have independent
sensing for all keys, but instead detect the overall
re by means of a sensing strip running beneath the keys.
ouch may be used to control musical functions such as
to depth, filter brightness, loudness and so on, though it
y also be used to control some parameter of a MIDI effects
iit, such as delay feedback or effect level.

algorithm
Computer program designed to perform a specific task. In the
context of effects units, algorithms usually describe a software
building block designed to create a specific effect or combination
of effects. All digital effects are based on algorithms.

ambience
The result of sound reflections in a confined space being
added to the original sound. Ambience may also be created
electronically by some digital reverb units. The main difference
between ambience and reverberation is that ambience doesn't
have the characteristic long delay time of reverberation – the
reflections mainly give the sound a sense of space.

amplifier
Device that increases the level of an electrical signal.

amplitude
Another word for level. Refers to sound or electrical signal.

analogue

Circuitry that uses a continually-changing voltage or current to represent a signal. The origin of the term is that the electrical signal can be thought of as being analogous to the original signal.

attack

Time taken for a sound to achieve maximum amplitude. Drums have a fast attack, whereas bowed strings have a slow attack. In compressors and gates, the attack time equates to how quickly the processor can change its gain.

attenuate

To make lower in level.

aux

Control on a mixing console designed to route a proportion of the channel signal to the effects or cue mix outputs.

aux return

Mixer inputs used to add effects to the mix.

aux send

Physical output from a mixer aux send buss.

balance

This word has several meanings in recording. It may refer to the relative levels of the left and right channels of a stereo recording, or it may be used to describe the relative levels of the various instruments and voices within a mix.

bandpass

Filter that passes frequencies only between specific upper and lower limits.

bandpass filter (BDF)

Filter that removes or attenuates frequencies above and below the frequency at which it is set. Frequencies within the band are emphasised. Bandpass filters are often used in synthesisers as tone-shaping elements.

bandwidth

Means of specifying the range of frequencies passed by an electronic circuit such as an amplifier, mixer or filter. The frequency range is usually measured at the points where the level drops by 3dB relative to the maximum.

binary

Counting system based on only two numbers: 1 and 0.

bios

Part of a computer operating system held on ROM rather than on disk. This handles basic routines such as accessing the disk drive.

bit

Binary digit, which may either be 1 or 0.

boost/cut control

single control which allows the range of frequencies passing through a filter to be either amplified or attenuated. The centre position is usually the 'flat' or 'no effect' position.

bouncing

Process of mixing two or more recorded tracks together and

re-recording these onto another track.

BPM

Beats Per Minute.

breath controller

Device that converts breath pressure into MIDI controller data.

bug

Slang term for software fault or equipment design problem.

buss

Common electrical signal path along which signals may travel. In a mixer, there are several busses carrying the stereo mix, the groups, the PFL signal, the aux sends and so on. Power supplies are also fed along busses.

byte

Piece of digital data comprising eight bits.

cardioid

Meaning heart shaped, describes the polar response of a unidirectional microphone.

channel

Single strip of controls in a mixing console relating to either a single input or a pair of main/monitor inputs.

channel

In the context of MIDI, Channel refers to one of 16 possible data channels over which MIDI data may be sent. The organisation of data by channels means that up to 16 different MIDI instruments or parts may be addressed using a single cable.

channel
In the context of mixing consoles, a channel is a single strip of controls relating to one input.

chase
Term describing the process whereby a slave device attempts to synchronise itself with a master device. In the context of a MIDI sequence, Chase may also involve chasing events – looking back to earlier positions in the song to see if there are any program changes or other events that need to be acted upon.

chip
Integrated circuit.

chord
Two or more different musical notes played at the same time.

chorus
Effect created by doubling a signal and adding delay and pitch modulation.

chromatic
Scale of pitches rising in steps of one semitone .

click track
Metronome pulse which helps musicians to keep time.

clipping

Severe form of distortion which occurs when a signal attempts to exceed the maximum level which a piece of equipment can handle.

clone

Exact duplicate. Often refers to digital copies of digital tapes.

common-mode rejection

Measure of how well a balanced circuit rejects a signal that is common to both inputs.

compander

Encode/decode device that compresses a signal while encoding it, then expands it when decoding it.

compressor

Device designed to reduce the dynamic range of audio signals by reducing the level of high signals or by increasing the level of low signals.

computer

Device for the storing and processing of digital data.

conductor

Material that provides a low resistance path for electrical current.

console

Alternative term for mixer.

contact enhancer

Compound designed to increase the electrical conductivity

of electrical contacts such as plugs, sockets and edge connectors.

continuous controller
Type of MIDI message used to translate continuous change, such as from a pedal, wheel or breath control device.

copy protection
Method used by software manufacturers to prevent unauthorised copying.

crash
Slang term relating to malfunction of a computer program.

cut-and-paste editing
Copying or moving sections of a recording to different locations.

cutoff frequency
Frequency above or below which attenuation begins in a filter circuit.

cycle
One complete vibration of a sound source or its electrical equivalent. One cycle per second is expressed as one Hertz (Hz).

CV
Control Voltage. Used to control the pitch of an oscillator or filter frequency in an analogue synthesiser. Most analogue synthesisers follow a one volt per octave convention, though there are exceptions. To use a pre-MIDI analogue synthesiser under MIDI control, a MIDI-to-CV converter is required.

daisy chain

Term used to describe serial electrical connection between devices or modules.

damping

In the context of reverberation, damping refers to the rate at which reverberant energy is absorbed by the various surfaces in an environment.

DAT

Digital Audio Tape. The most commonly-used DAT machines are more correctly known as R-DATs because they use a rotating head similar to that in a video recorder. Digital recorders using fixed or stationary heads (such as DCC) are known as S-DAT machines.

data

Information stored and used by a computer.

data compression

System for reducing the amount of data stored by a digital system. Most audio data compression systems are known as lossy systems, as some of the original signal is discarded in accordance with psychoacoustic principles designed to ensure that only components which cannot be heard are lost.

dB

Decibel. Unit used to express the relative levels of two electrical voltages, powers or sounds.

dBm

Variation on dB referenced to 0dB = 1mW into 600 ohms.

dBv

Variation on dB referenced to 0dB = 0.775v.

dBV

Variation on dB referenced to 0dB = 1V.

dB/octave

A means of measuring the slope of a filter. The more decibels per octave the sharper the filter slope.

dbx

A commercial encode/decode tape noise reduction system that compresses the signal during recording and expands it by an identical amount on playback.

DC

Direct Current.

DCC

Stationary-head digital recorder format developed by Philips. Uses a data-compression system to reduce the amount of data that needs to be stored.

DCO

Digitally-Controlled Oscillator.

decay

Progressive reduction in amplitude of a sound or electrical signal over time. In the context of an ADSR envelope shaper, the decay phase starts as soon as the attack phase has reached its maximum level. In the decay phase, the signal level drops until it reaches the sustain level set by the user. The signal then remains at this level until the key is released, at which point the release phase is entered.

de-esser
Device designed to reduce the effect of sibilance in vocal signals.

DI
Direct Inject, in which a signal is plugged directly into an audio chain without the aid of a microphone.

DI box
Device for matching the signal-level impedance of a source to a tape machine or mixer input.

digital
Electronic system which represents data and signals in the form of codes comprising 1s and 0s.

digital delay
Digital processor for generating delay and echo effects.

digital reverb
Digital processor for simulating reverberation.

DIN connector
Consumer multi-pin signal connection format, also used for MIDI cabling. Various pin configurations are available.

direct coupling
Means of connecting two electrical circuits so that both AC and DC signals may be passed between them.

disc

Used to describe vinyl discs, CDs and MiniDiscs.

disk

Abbreviation of diskette, but now used to describe computer floppy, hard and removable disks (see Floppy Disk).

dither

System of adding low-level noise to a digitised audio signal in such a way that extends the low-level resolution at the expense of a slight deterioration in noise performance.

DMA

Direct Memory Access. Part of a computer operating system that allows peripheral devices to communicate directly with the memory without going via the CPU (Central Processing Unit).

Dolby

An encode/decode tape noise reduction system that amplifies low-level, high-frequency signals during recording, then reverses this process during playback. There are several different Dolby systems in use, including types B, C and S for domestic and semi-professional machines, and types A and SR for professional machines. Recordings made whilst using one of these systems must also be replayed via the same system.

DOS

Disk Operating System. Part of the operating system of PC and PC-compatible computers.

driver

Piece of software that handles communications between the

main program and a hardware peripheral, such as a soundcard, printer or scanner.

drum pad
Synthetic playing surface which produces electronic trigger signals in response to being hit with drumsticks.

dry
Signal to which no effects have been added. Conversely, a sound which has been treated with an effect, such as reverberation, is referred to as wet.

DSP
Digital Signal Processor. A powerful microchip used to process digital signals.

dubbing
Adding further material to an existing recording. Also known as overdubbing.

ducking
System for controlling the level of one audio signal with another. For example, background music can be made to duck whenever there is a voice-over.

dump
To transfer digital data from one device to another. A Sysex dump is a means of transmitting information about a particular instrument or module over MIDI, and may be used to store sound patches, parameter settings and so on.

dynamic microphone

Type of microphone that works on the electric generator principle, whereby a diaphragm moves a coil of wire within a magnetic field.

dynamic range
Range in decibels between the highest signal that can be handled by a piece of equipment and the level at which small signals disappear into the noise floor.

dynamics
Method of describing the relative levels within a piece of music.

early reflections
First sound reflections from walls, floors and ceilings following a sound which is created in an acoustically reflective environment.

effects loop
Connection system that allows an external signal processor to be connected into the audio chain.

effects return
Additional mixer input designed to accommodate the output from an effects unit.

effects unit
Device for treating an audio signal in order to change it in some creative way. Effects often involve the use of delay circuits, and include such treatments as reverb and echo.

encode/decode
System that requires a signal to be processed prior to recording, which is then reversed during playback.

enhancer

Device designed to brighten audio material using techniques such as dynamic equalisation, phase shifting and harmonic generation.

envelope

The way in which the level of a sound or signal varies over time.

envelope generator

Circuit capable of generating a control signal which represents the envelope of the sound you want to recreate. This may then be used to control the level of an oscillator or other sound source, though envelopes may also be used to control filter or modulation settings. The most common example is the ADSR generator.

equaliser

Device for selectively cutting or boosting selected parts of the audio spectrum.

erase

To remove recorded material from an analogue tape, or to remove digital data from any form of storage medium.

event

In MIDI terms, an event is a single unit of MIDI data, such as a note being turned on or off, a piece of controller information, a program change, and so on.

exciter

Enhancer that works by synthesising new high-frequency harmonics.

expander

Device designed to decrease the level of low-level signals and increase the level of high-level signals, thus increasing the dynamic range of the signal.

expander module

Synthesiser with no keyboard, often rack mountable or in some other compact format.

fader

Sliding potentiometer control used in mixers and other processors.

FET

Field Effect Transistor.

figure-of-eight

Describes the polar response of a microphone that is equally sensitive at both front and rear, yet rejects sounds coming from the sides.

file

Meaningful list of data stored in digitally. A Standard MIDI File is a specific type of file designed to allow sequence information to be exchanged between different types of sequencer.

filter

Electronic circuit designed to emphasise or attenuate a specific range of frequencies.

flanging

Modulated delay effect using feedback to create a dramatic, sweeping sound.

floppy disk
Computer disk that uses a flexible magnetic medium encased in a protective plastic sleeve. The maximum capacity of a standard high-density disk is 1.44Mb. Earlier double-density disks hold only around half the amount of data.

flutter echo
Resonant echo that occurs when sound reflects back and forth between two parallel reflective surfaces.

foldback
System for feeding one or more separate mixes to the performers for use while recording and overdubbing. Also known as a cue mix.

format
Procedure required to ready a computer disk for use. Formatting organises the disk's surface into a series of electronic pigeonholes into which data can be stored. Different computers often use different formatting systems.

frequency
Indication of how many cycles of a repetitive waveform occur in one second. A waveform which has a repetition cycle of once per second has a frequency of 1Hz.

frequency response
Measurement of the frequency range that can be handled by a specific piece of electrical equipment or loudspeaker.

FSK
Frequency-Shift Keying. A method of recording a sync clock signal onto tape by representing it as two alternating tones.

fundamental
Any sound comprises a fundamental or basic frequency plus harmonics and partials at a higher frequency.

gain
Amount by which a circuit amplifies a signal.

gate
Electrical signal that is generated whenever a key is depressed on an electronic keyboard. This is used to trigger envelope generators and other events that need to be synchronised to key action.

gate
Electronic device designed to mute low-level signals, thus improving the noise performance during pauses in the wanted material.

general MIDI
Addition to the basic MIDI spec to assure a minimum level of compatibility when playing back GM-format song files. The specification covers type and program, number of sounds, minimum levels of polyphony and multitimbrality, response to controller information and so on.

GM reset
Universal Sysex command which activates the General MIDI mode on a GM instrument. The same command also sets all

controllers to their default values and switches off any notes still playing by means of an All Notes Off message.

ground

Electrical earth, or zero volts. In mains wiring, the ground cable is physically connected to the ground via a long conductive metal spike.

group

Collection of signals within a mixer that are mixed and then routed through a separate fader to provide overall control. In a multitrack mixer, several groups are provided to feed the various recorder track inputs.

GS

Roland's own extension to the General MIDI protocol.

hard disk

High-capacity computer storage device based on a rotating rigid disk with a magnetic coating onto which data may be recorded.

harmonic

High-frequency component of a complex waveform.

harmonic distortion

Addition of harmonics not present in the original signal.

head

Part of a tape machine or disk drive that reads and/or writes data to and from the storage media.

Hz

Shorthand for Hertz, the unit of frequency.

IC
Integrated Circuit.

impedance
Can be visualised as the AC resistance of a circuit which contains both resistive and reactive components.

inductor
Reactive component which presents an impedance with increases with frequency.

insert point
Connector that allows an external processor to be patched into a signal path so that the signal then flows through it.

insulator
Material that does not conduct electricity.

interface
Device that acts as an intermediary to two or more other pieces of equipment. For example, a MIDI interface enables a computer to communicate with MIDI instruments and keyboards.

I/O
The part of a system that handles inputs and outputs, usually in the digital domain.

jack
Commonly-used audio connector. May be either mono (TS) or stereo (TRS).

k

Abbreviation for 1000 (kilo). Used as a prefix to other values to indicate magnitude.

LCD

Liquid Crystal Display.

LED

Solid-state lamp.

LSB

Least Significant Byte. If a piece of data has to be conveyed as two bytes, one byte represents high-value numbers and the other low-value numbers, in the same way that tens and units function in the decimal system. The high value, or most significant part of the message, is called the Most Significant Byte or MSB.

limiter

Device that controls the gain of a signal so as to prevent it from ever exceeding a preset level. A limiter is essentially a fast-acting compressor with an infinite compression ratio.

line level

Mixers and signal processors tend to work at a standard signal level known as line level. In practice there are several different standard line levels, but all are in the order of a few volts. A nominal signal level is around -10dBv for semi-pro equipment and +4dBv for professional equipment.

load

Electrical circuit that draws power from another circuit or power supply. Also describes reading data into a computer.

load on/off
Function to allow the keyboard and sound-generating section of a keyboard synthesiser to be used independently of each other.

loop
Circuit where the output is connected back to the input.

low-frequency oscillator (LFO)
Oscillator used as a modulation source, usually below 20Hz. The most common LFO waveshape is the sine wave, though there is often a choice of sine, square, triangular and sawtooth waveforms.

mA
Milliamp, or one thousandth of an amp.

MDM
Modular Digital Multitrack. A digital recorder that can be used in multiples to provide a greater number of synchronised tracks than a single machine.

memory
Computer's RAM memory used to store programs and data. This data is lost when the computer is switched off and so must be stored to disk or other suitable media.

menu
List of choices presented by a computer program or a device with a display window.

mic level

Low-level signal generated by a microphone. This must be amplified many times to increase it to line level.

microprocessor
Specialised microchip at the heart of a computer. It is here that instructions are read and acted upon.

MIDI
Musical Instrument Digital Interface.

MIDI analyser
Device that gives a visual readout of MIDI activity when connected between two pieces of MIDI equipment.

MIDI bank change
Type of controller message used to select alternate banks of MIDI programs where access to more than 128 programs is required.

MIDI controller
Term used to describe the physical interface by means of which the musician plays the MIDI synthesiser or other sound generator. Examples of controllers are keyboards, drum pads, wind synths and so on.

MIDI control change
Also known as MIDI Controllers or Controller Data. These messages convey positional information relating to performance controls such as wheels, pedals, switches and other devices. This information can be used to control functions such as vibrato depth, brightness, portamento, effects levels, and many other parameters.

(standard) MIDI file

Standard file format for storing song data recorded on a MIDI sequencer in such as way as to allow it to be read by other makes or models of MIDI sequencer.

MIDI implementation chart

A chart, usually found in MIDI product manuals, which provides information as to which MIDI features are supported. Supported features are marked with a 0 while unsupported feature are marked with a X. Additional information may be provided, such as the exact form of the bank change message.

MIDI in

The socket used to receive information from a master controller or from the MIDI Thru socket of a slave unit.

MIDI merge

Device or sequencer function that enables two or more streams of MIDI data to be combined.

MIDI mode

MIDI information can be interpreted by the receiving MIDI instrument in a number of ways, the most common being polyphonically on a single MIDI channel (poly-omni off mode). Omni mode enables a MIDI Instrument to play all incoming data regardless of channel.

MIDI module

Sound-generating device with no integral keyboard.

MIDI note number

Every key on a MIDI keyboard has its own note number,

ranging from 0 to 127, where 60 represents middle C. Some systems use C3 as middle C while others use C4.

MIDI note off
MIDI message sent when key is released.

MIDI note on
Message sent when note is pressed.

MIDI out
MIDI connector used to send data from a master device to the MIDI In of a connected slave device.

MIDI port
MIDI connections of a MIDI-compatible device. A multiport, in the context of a MIDI interface, is a device with multiple MIDI output sockets, each capable of carrying data relating to a different set of 16 MIDI channels. Multiports are the only means of exceeding the limitations imposed by 16 MIDI channels.

MIDI program change
Type of MIDI message used to change sound patches on a remote module or the effects patch on a MIDI effects unit.

MIDI splitter
Alternative term for MIDI thru box.

MIDI sync
Description of the synchronisation systems available to MIDI users: MIDI Clock and MIDI Time Code.

MIDI thru

Socket on a slave unit used to feed the MIDI In socket of the next unit in line.

MIDI thru box
Device which splits the MIDI Out signal of a master instrument or sequencer to avoid daisy chaining. Powered circuitry is used to 'buffer' the outputs so as to prevent problems when many pieces of equipment are driven from a single MIDI output.

mixer
Device for combining two or more audio signals.

monitor
Reference loudspeaker used for mixing.

monitor
VDU for a computer.

monitoring
Action of listening to a mix or a specific audio signal.

monophonic
One note at a time.

MTC
MIDI Time Code. A MIDI sync implementation based on SMPTE time code.

multitimbral module
MIDI sound source capable of producing several different sounds at the same time and controlled on different MIDI channels.

multitrack

Recording device capable of recording several 'parallel' parts or tracks which may then be mixed or re-recorded independently.

noise reduction

System for reducing analogue tape noise or for reducing the level of hiss present in a recording.

noise shaping

System for creating digital dither so that any added noise is shifted into those parts of the audio spectrum where the human ear is least sensitive.

non-registered parameter number

Addition to the basic MIDI spec that allows controllers 98 and 99 to be used to control non-standard parameters relating to particular models of synthesiser. This is an alternative to using system-exclusive data to achieve the same ends, though NRPNs tend to be used mainly by Yamaha and Roland instruments.

octave

When a frequency or pitch is transposed up by one octave, its frequency is doubled.

off-line

Process carried out while a recording is not playing. For example, some computer-based processes have to be carried out off-line as the computer isn't fast enough to carry out the process in real time.

omni

Refers to a microphone that is equally sensitive in all directions, or to the MIDI mode in which data on all channels is recognised.

oscillator
Circuit which is designed to generate a periodic electrical waveform.

overdub
To add another part to a multitrack recording or to replace one of the existing parts (see Dubbing).

pad
Resistive circuit for reducing signal level.

parallel
Method of connecting two or more circuits together so that their inputs and outputs are all connected together.

parameter
Variable value that affects some aspect of a device's performance.

parametric EQ
Equaliser with separate controls for frequency, bandwidth and cut/boost.

patch
Alternative term for program. Referring to a single programmed sound within a synthesiser that can be called up using program-change commands. MIDI effects units and samplers also have patches.

patch bay
System of panel-mounted connectors used to bring inputs and outputs to a central point from where they can be routed using plug-in patch cords.

patch cord
Short cable used with patch bays.

peak
The highest signal level in any section of programme material, or the maximum instantaneous level of a signal.

PFL
Pre-Fade Listen. A system used within a mixing console to allow the operator to listen in on a selected signal, regardless of the position of the fader controlling that signal.

phase
Timing difference between two electrical waveforms expressed in degrees where 360° corresponds to a delay of exactly one cycle.

phaser
Effect which combines a signal with a phase-shifted version of itself to produce creative filtering effects. Most phasers are controlled by means of an LFO.

pickup
Part of a guitar that converts string vibrations to electrical signals.

pitch
Musical interpretation of an audio frequency.

pitch bend

Special control message specifically designed to produce a change in pitch in response to the movement of a pitch bend wheel or lever. Pitch bend data can be recorded and edited, just like any other MIDI controller data, even though it isn't part of the controller message group.

pitch shifter

Device for changing the pitch of an audio signal without changing its duration.

polyphony

An instrument's ability to play two or more notes simultaneously. An instrument which can play only one note at a time is described as monophonic.

poly mode

The most common MIDI mode, which allows any instrument to respond to multiple simultaneous notes transmitted on a single MIDI channel.

port

Connection for the input or output of data.

portamento

Gliding effect that allows a sound to change pitch at a gradual rate rather than abruptly when a new key is pressed or MIDI note sent.

post-fade

Aux signal taken from after the channel fader so that the aux send level follows any channel fader changes. Normally used for feeding effects devices.

PPM
Peak Programme Meter. A meter designed to register signal peaks rather than the average level.

PPQN
Pulsed Per Quarter Note. Used in the context of MIDI clock-derived sync signals.

pre-fade
Aux signal taken from before the channel fader so that the channel fader has no effect on the aux send level. Normally used for creating foldback or cue mixes.

preset
Effects unit or synth patch that cannot be altered by the user.

pressure
Alternative term for aftertouch.

processor
Device designed to treat an audio signal by changing its dynamics or frequency content. Examples of processors include compressors, gates and equalisers.

program change
MIDI message designed to change instrument or effects unit patches.

quantising
Means of moving notes recorded in a MIDI sequencer so that

they line up with user defined subdivisions of a musical bar – 16s, for example. The facility may be used to correct timing errors, but over-quantising can remove the human feel from a performance.

RAM
Abbreviation for Random Access Memory. This is a type of memory used by computers for the temporary storage of programs and data, and all data is lost when the power is turned off. For that reason, work needs to be saved to disk if it is not to be lost.

real time
Audio process that can be carried out as the signal is being recorded or played back. The opposite is off-line, where the signal is processed in non-real time.

release
Time taken for a level or gain to return to normal. Often used to describe the rate at which a synthesised sound reduces in level after a key has been released.

resistance
Opposition to the flow of electrical current. Measured in ohms.

resolution
Accuracy with which an analogue signal is represented by a digitising system. The more bits are used, the more accurately the amplitude of each sample can be measured, but there are other elements of converter design that also affect accuracy. High conversion accuracy is known as high resolution.

resonance

Same as Q.

reverb

Acoustic ambience created by multiple reflections in a confined space.

RF

Radio Frequency.

RF interference

Interference significantly above the range of human hearing.

release

Rate at which a signal amplitude decays once a key has been released.

resonance

Characteristic of a filter that allows it to selectively pass a narrow range of frequencies (see Q).

roll-off

The rate at which a filter attenuates a signal once it has passed the filter cutoff point.

ROM

Abbreviation for Read-Only Memory. This is a permanent and non-volatile type of memory containing data that can't be changed. Operating systems are often stored on ROM as the memory remains intact when the power is switched off.

sample

Process carried out by an A/D converter where the instantaneous amplitude of a signal is measured many times per second (44.1kHz in the case of CD).

sample
Digitised sound used as a musical sound source in a sampler or additive synthesiser.

sample rate
Number of times which an A/D converter samples the incoming waveform each second.

sequencer
Device for recording and replaying MIDI data, usually in a multitrack format, allowing complex compositions to be built up a part at a time.

side chain
Part of acircuit that splits off a proportion of the main signal to be processed in some way. Compressors uses aside-chain signal to derive their control signals.

signal chain
Route taken by a signal from the input of a system to its output.

signal-to-noise ratio
Ratio of maximum signal level to the residual noise, expressed in decibels.

slave
Device under the control of a master device.

SMPTE
Time code developed for the film industry but now extensively used in music and recording. SMPTE is a real-time code and is related to hours, minutes, seconds and film or video frames rather than to musical tempo.

SPP
Song-Position Pointer (MIDI).

standard MIDI file
Standard file format that allows MIDI files to be transferred between different sequencers and MIDI file players.

step time
System for programming a sequencer in non-real time.

stereo
Two-channel system feeding left and right loudspeakers.

subtractive synthesis
Process of creating a new sound by filtering and shaping a raw, harmonically complex waveform.

sustain
Part of the ADSR envelope which determines the level to which the sound will settle if a key is held down. Once the key is released, the sound decays at a rate set by the release parameter. Also refers to a guitar's ability to hold notes which decay very slowly.

sync
System for making two or more pieces of equipment run in

synchronism with each other.

synthesiser
Electronic musical instrument designed to create a wide range of sounds, both imitative and abstract.

tempo
Rate of the beat of a piece of music, measured here in BPM.

thru
MIDI connector which passes on the signal received at the MIDI In socket.

timbre
Tonal 'colour' of a sound.

track
This term dates back to multitrack tape, on which the tracks are physical stripes of recorded material located side by side along the length of the tape.

tracking
System whereby one device follows another. Tracking is often discussed in the context of MIDI guitar synthesisers or controllers where the MIDI output attempts to track the pitch of the guitar strings.

transpose
To shift a musical signal by a fixed number of semitones.

tremolo
Modulation of the amplitude of a sound using an LFO.

TRS jack

Stereo-type jack with tip, ring and sleeve connections.

unison

To play the same melody using two or more different instruments or voices.

velocity

The rate at which a key is depressed. This may be used to control loudness (to simulate the response of instruments such as pianos) or other parameters on later synthesisers.

vibrato

Pitch modulation using an LFO to modulate a VCO.

voice

Capacity of a synthesiser to play a single musical note. An instrument capable of playing 16 simultaneous notes is said to be a 16-voice instrument.

volt

Unit of electrical power.

XG

Yamaha's alternative to Roland's GS system for enhancing the General MIDI protocol so as to provide additional banks of patches and further editing facilities.

Y-lead

Lead split so that one source can feed two destinations. Y-leads may also be used in console insert points, when a stereo jack plug at one end of the lead is split into two monos at the other.